# Bible Stories
# AMIGURUMI

16 INSPIRATIONAL CROCHET PROJECTS

BIANCA SANTOS

weldonowen

*To my mom, Rosana,
my aunt Elizete, and my
mother-in-law, Melanie,
three incredible women
of faith. I know this book
will mean as much to you
as it does to me.*

# Contents

# Introduction

Since I was a child, Bible stories have always felt like more than stories. They were lessons, comfort, and imagination all at once, powerful stories told through faith, family, and connection. I remember listening with curiosity and wonder, picturing every moment so clearly that I could almost see the characters in front of me. Those memories stayed with me throughout my life.

Years later, when I found amigurumi, I felt that same spark of wonder. Crochet became a way to quiet the world around me, to return to peace, and to create something filled with purpose. Every stitch is slow, intentional, and grounding, and in many ways, that process reminds me of faith itself.

While working on this book, I returned to those stories: Each character carries not only yarn and stuffing, but also meaning, courage, forgiveness, obedience, hope, resilience, and love. From Adam and Eve to Moses, Noah, Daniel, David, and Samson, each one represents a moment that has touched generations across time, culture, and language.

Crochet has been many things for me: my therapy, my creative outlet, my profession, and a dream come true. Bringing these biblical stories to life through amigurumi felt like a celebration of everything I love: faith, storytelling, teaching, and handmade art. Every project in these pages was created with care, intention, and heart. I hope that you not only enjoy crocheting them, but also feel the deeper meaning they carry.

Whether you're making these pieces for yourself, a loved one, a child, a church group, or simply because you love the stories, I hope they bring joy and connection to your life and home. Crochet is a beautiful way to create memories and stories made by hand that stay with us forever.

Now it's your turn: grab your hook, choose your first story, and let every stitch bring these timeless characters to life with your own hands.

# In the Beginning

# The Story of Adam and Eve

**Genesis 2:4–3:24**

**The story of Adam and Eve is one of the most well-known in the Bible. God created Adam and put him in the Garden of Eden to tend and keep it, telling Adam that he may eat from any tree in the garden except the tree of knowledge. Seeing that Adam needed a companion, God took a rib from Adam's side and created Eve. Our amigurumis illustrate the next part of the story:**

> Now the serpent was more subtil than any beast of the field which the Lord God
> had made. And he said unto the woman, Yea, hath God said, Ye shall not eat of
> every tree of the garden?[1] And the woman said unto the serpent, We may eat of
> the fruit of the trees of the garden:[2] But of the fruit of the tree which is in the midst
> of the garden, God hath said, Ye shall not eat of it, neither shall ye touch it, lest ye
> die.[3] And the serpent said unto the woman, Ye shall not surely die:[4] For God doth
> know that in the day ye eat thereof, then your eyes shall be opened, and ye shall
> be as gods, knowing good and evil.[5] And when the woman saw that the tree was
> good for food, and that it was pleasant to the eyes, and a tree to be desired to
> make one wise, she took of the fruit thereof, and did eat, and gave also unto her
> husband with her; and he did eat.[6] And the eyes of them both were opened, and
> they knew that they were naked; and they sewed fig leaves together, and made
> themselves aprons.[7]

**—Genesis 3:1–7**

God learns of their partaking of the forbidden fruit and curses the serpent, then banishes Adam and Eve from the garden of Eden, placing cherubim at the east of the Garden and a flaming sword to protect the tree of life.

# Eve and the Apple

## YARN

Fingering weight (#1 super fine) yarn, shown in Scheepjes *Catona* (100% mercerized cotton, 174 yd. / 125 m per 1.75 oz. / 50 g ball)

**SKIN**

255 Shell

**LEAF/OUTFIT/TIARA**

412 Forest Green

**HAIR**

162 Black Coffee

**EYE DETAIL**

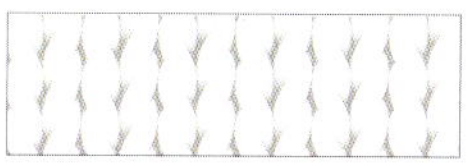

106 Snow White

Any standard brown embroidery thread can be used for the eyebrows and eyelashes.

## FOR THE APPLE

Fingering weight (#1 super fine) yarn, shown in Scheepjes *Catona* (100% mercerized cotton, 174 yd. / 125 m per 1.75 oz. / 50 g ball)

**APPLE**

114 Hot Red

**LEAF**

412 Forest Green

## FINISHED MEASUREMENTS

### EVE

**HEIGHT:** 5.5 in. / 14 cm
**WIDTH:** 2.75 in. / 7 cm

### APPLE

**HEIGHT:** 1 in. / 2.5 cm

## HOOK

- US B-1 / 2.0 mm crochet hook for the Apple and Eve's Body, Skirt, and Accessories
- US C-2 / 2.5 mm crochet hook for the Hair

***Note:*** *Everything is worked with US B-1 / 2.0 mm crochet hook except for the Hair.*

## NOTIONS

- Pair of 13 mm safety eyes
- Polyester stuffing
- Removable stitch markers
- Tapestry needle
- Sewing pins
- Pointy tweezers
- Craft glue
- Makeup blush (optional)

## GAUGE

*Gauge is not critical for this project. Ensure your stitches are tight so the stuffing won't show through.*

For more information on how to make Eve and the Apple, including tips, step-by-step pictures, and videos, scan this QR code!

## HEAD

With **Shell**.
**Rnd 1:** 6 sc in magic ring
**Rnd 2:** 6 inc [12]
**Rnd 3:** (1 sc, 1 inc) × 6 [18]
**Rnd 4:** 1 sc, 1 inc, (2 sc, 1 inc) × 5, 1 sc [24]
**Rnd 5:** (3 sc, 1 inc) × 6 [30]
**Rnd 6:** 2 sc, 1 inc, (4 sc, 1 inc) × 5, 2 sc [36]
**Rnd 7:** (5 sc, 1 inc) × 6 [42]
**Rnd 8:** 3 sc, 1 inc, (6 sc, 1 inc) × 5, 3 sc [48]
**Rnd 9:** 48 sc
**Rnd 10:** (5 sc, 1 inc) × 8 [56]
**Rnds 11–22:** 56 sc (12 rounds)
Insert the eyes between rounds 17 and 18, with 8 sc visible apart from each other.
**Rnd 23:** (5 sc, 1 dec) × 8 [48]
**Rnd 24:** 2 sc, 1 dec, (4 sc, 1 dec) × 7, 2 sc [40]
**Rnd 25:** 1 sc, 1 dec, (2 sc, 1 dec) × 9, 1 sc [30]
**Rnd 26:** (1 sc, 1 dec) × 10 [20]
Stuff the Head until round 26. You should not stuff from round 27 on.
**Rnd 27:** Blo 20 sc
**Rnds 28–35:** 20 sc (8 rounds)
**Rnd 36:** 10 dec [10]
Fasten off with an inverted magic ring.
Push the neck inward (from round 27 to 36) with the help of the hook handle.
For more instructions, see page 167.

## EARS (MAKE 2)

With **Shell**, make a magic ring.
**Rnd 1:** In ring: 1 sc, 4 hdc, 1 sc
Finish off and leave a long thread to sew.

## NOSE

With **Shell**.
Embroider the Nose between **rounds 18** and **19**, leaving **3 sc** away from the eyes. Pass the yarn horizontally **2 times** at a distance of **2 sc**. Then, pass the same yarn several times vertically and fasten off.

## EYEBROWS (MAKE 2)

With brown embroidery thread, make the Eyebrows with their outer corner 1 round above the eyes and the inner corner 2 rounds above the eyes, with a width of 4 sc.

## LEFT LEG

With **Shell**.
Working on both sides of the chains. Start with 5 chains and from the second chain from the hook make:
**Rnd 1:** 1 inc, 2 sc, in the last chain 4 sc, continue on the other side of the chains 2 sc, 1 inc [12]
**Rnd 2:** 2 inc, 2 sc, 4 inc, 2 sc, 2 inc [20]
**Rnd 3:** 20 BPsc
**Rnd 4:** 20 sc
**Rnd 5:** 6 sc, 4 dec, 6 sc [16]
**Rnd 6:** 5 sc, 3 dec, 5 sc [13]
**Rnds 7–13:** 13 sc (7 rounds)
Stuff the Leg and fasten off.
If you want your amigurumi to have flat feet to stand, make sure that you don't stuff it too much and leave it concave.

## RIGHT LEG AND BODY

Repeat rounds 1 to 13 of the Left Leg.
Make **4 more sc** and **2 chains** to get to the side of the Leg. Be sure that both feet are facing forward at the junction of the Legs.
**Rnd 14:** 13 sc, 2 sc on the chain, 13 sc, 2 sc on the chain [30]
**Rnds 15–18:** 30 sc (4 rounds)
**Rnd 19:** (13 sc, 1 dec) × 2 [28]
**Rnd 20:** 28 sc
**Rnd 21:** 6 sc, 1 dec, 12 sc, 1 dec, 6 sc [26]
**Rnd 22:** Change to **Forest Green**. (11 sc, 1 dec) × 2 [24]
**Rnd 23:** 24 sc
**Rnd 24:** 5 sc, 1 dec, 10 sc, 1 dec, 5 sc [22]
**Rnd 25:** Change to **Shell**. Blo (9 sc, 1 dec) × 2 [20]
**Rnd 26:** 20 sc
**Rnd 27:** 4 sc, 1 dec, 8 sc, 1 dec, 4 sc [18]
**Rnds 28–34:** 18 sc (7 rounds)
**Rnd 35:** 9 dec [9]
Stuff the Body and leave a long tail to sew.

## BOTTOM OF THE TOP

With **Forest Green**.
Insert the hook between rounds 21 and 22. Crochet between the stitches (we will use the gaps between stitches). Make 26 sl st and fasten off.

## UPPER PART OF THE TOP

With **Forest Green**.
Working on the back loops from round 25, make:
(1 sl st, 1 chain) × 22 – Fasten off.

## ARMS (MAKE 2)

With **Shell**.

**Rnd 1:** 6 sc in magic ring

**Rnd 2:** (2 sc, 1 inc) × 2 [8]

**Rnds 3–9:** 8 sc (7 rounds)

Stuff half of the Arms (until round 5).

Pinch Arm opening closed and crochet together with 4 sc. Leave a long tail.

## HAIR

With **Black Coffee** and US C-2 / 2.5 mm hook.

**Rnd 1:** 8 sc in magic ring

**Rnd 2:** 8 inc [16]

**Rnd 3:** (1 sc, 1 inc) × 8 [24]

**Rnd 4:** 1 sc, 1 inc, (2 sc, 1 inc) × 7, 1 sc [32]

**Rnd 5:** (3 sc, 1 inc) × 8 [40]

**Rnd 6:** 2 sc, 1 inc, (4 sc, 1 inc) × 7, 2 sc [48]

Now we will work around the 48 sc of round 6 to make the Hair strands. Make 1 sl st between each strand of Hair.

**Strnds 1–17:** 32 chains, and from the third chain make 30 hdc, sl st in the next st. (Remember to add 1 more sl st between each strand.)

**Strnd 18:** 10 chains, and from the third chain make 8 hdc, sl st in the next st.

**Strnd 19:** 13 chains, and from the third chain make 11 hdc, sl st in the next st.

**Strnd 20:** 1 sl st

**Strnd 21:** 19 chains, and from the third chain make 17 hdc, sl st in the next st.

**Strnd 22:** 16 chains, and from the third chain make 14 hdc, sl st in the next st.

**Strnd 23:** 13 chains, and from the third chain make 11 hdc, sl st in the next st.

**Strnd 24:** 10 chains, and from the third chain make 8 hdc, sl st in the next st.

## ROMANIAN LACE

To make the Tiara, follow the instructions below for Romanian Lace working with **Forest Green**.

**Note:** My Tiara measures 4 in. / 10 cm, but I advise checking it on the Head of your doll first before fastening it off.

You can learn this technique watching the video with the QR Code, or by following this step-by-step:

Make a slip knot and **2 chains**. From the second chain, make **1 sc**.

Turn the piece clockwise and insert the hook into the two loops on the left to make **1 sc**.

Repeat these 2 steps until it gets to the desired size (enough to form a Tiara on top of the Head).

## LEAVES FOR TIARA (MAKE 2)

With **Forest Green**.

Start with 6 chains. Work on both sides of the chains, and from the third chain make:

1 sc, 1 dc, 1 hdc, 3 sc in the same stitch, 1 hdc, 1 dc, 1 chain, 1 sl st

Leave a long tail.

## SKIRT

With **Forest Green**.

Start with 28 chains and close them in a ring with 1 sc. This is the first st of the round.

**Rnds 1–3:** 28 sc (3 rounds)

**Rnd 4:** (1 sl st, 5 chains and from the second chain from the hook 1 sc, 2 hdc, 1 dc. Skip 2 sc and 1 sl st in the following) × 7

**Note:** you should have 7 small triangles

**Rnd 5:** (1 sl st, 2 hdc, 2 sc, 2 chains, 1 sl st in the second chain from the hook, 2 sc, 2 hdc, 1 sl st) × 7

Fasten off.

Attach the yarn in the first loop of round 1, and make: (1 sl st, 1 chain) × 28

Fasten off.

## ASSEMBLY

Attach the Skirt to the Body.

Sew the Arms between rounds 25 and 26 on the side of the Body.

Using a tapestry needle attach the Head to the Body, pass the remaining tail of the Head and the remaining tail of the Body to the middle of the magic ring that started the Head.

Pull the two ends in order to adjust the Head to the Body, tie a knot and cut the tails. This way, the Head will be articulated.

Sew the Ears between rounds 16 and 18 (same line as the eyes), 3 sc apart from the eyes.

Embroider the eyelashes on top of the eyes with **Brown** embroidery thread.

Make the details on the outer corner of the eyes with **Snow White**, see page 164.

If you want the eyes to be indented, see the instructions on page 164.

Tip: I advise pinning every strand of Hair before applying glue. Just a drop of glue in each strand of Hair should be enough to fix it.

Place the Hair on the Head with the inverted side of the magic ring up.

Strands 18 to 24 should be placed above the Ears.

Strands 1 to 17 should be placed behind the Ears around the Head.

Place strand 19 to the right side of the Head, and strands 21 to 23 form the side bangs on the left.

Place the Tiara on top of the Head, just behind the bangs.

Sew the Leaves on top of the Tiara.

Apply some blush on her cheeks, just below the eyes.

## THE APPLE

With **Hot Red**.

**Rnd 1:** 8 sc in magic ring
**Rnd 2:** 8 inc [16]
**Rnd 3:** (3 sc, 1 inc) × 4 [20]
**Rnds 4–8:** 20 sc (5 rounds)
**Rnd 9:** (2 sc, 1 dec) × 5 [15]
**Rnd 10:** (1 sc, 1 dec) × 5 [10]
Stuff the Apple.
**Rnd 11:** 5 dec [5]

Fasten off with the inverted magic ring. Leave a long tail. Pass the tapestry needle through the middle of the inverted magic ring to the magic ring that started the Apple. Pull the yarn, in order to shrink the inverted magic ring, and tighten it with an invisible knot.

## LEAF

With **Forest Green**.

Start with 6 chains. Work on both sides of the chains, and from the third chain make:

1 sc, 1 dc, 1 hdc, 3 sc in the same stitch, 1 hdc, 1 dc, 1 sc, 1 chain, 1 sl st.

Leave a long tail.

## ASSEMBLY

Pass the remaining yarn of the Leaf through the middle of the inverted magic ring. Tie a knot and fasten off.

# Adam

## YARN

Fingering weight (#1 super fine) yarn, shown in Scheepjes *Catona* (100% mercerized cotton, 174 yd. / 125 m per 1.75 oz. / 50 g ball)

**SKIN**

255 Shell

**OUTFIT**

412 Forest Green

**STRIP**

157 Root Beer

**HAIR**

162 Black Coffee

**EYE DETAIL**

106 Snow White

Lace yarn (#0 lace) in brown color. Any standard brown embroidery thread can be used for the eyebrows.

## FINISHED MEASUREMENTS

**HEIGHT:** 5.5 in. / 14 cm
**WIDTH:** 2.75 in. / 7 cm

## HOOK

- US B-1 / 2.0 mm crochet hook

## NOTIONS

- Pair of 13 mm safety eyes
- Polyester stuffing
- Tapestry needle
- Removable stitch markers
- Sewing pins
- Pointy tweezers
- Craft glue

## GAUGE

*Gauge is not critical for this project. Ensure your stitches are tight so the stuffing won't show through.*

For more information on how to make Adam, including tips, step-by-step pictures, and videos, scan this QR code!

### HEAD

With **Shell**.
**Rnd 1:** 6 sc in magic ring
**Rnd 2:** 6 inc [12]
**Rnd 3:** (1 sc, 1 inc) × 6 [18]
**Rnd 4:** 1 sc, 1 inc, (2 sc, 1 inc) × 5, 1 sc [24]
**Rnd 5:** (3 sc, 1 inc) × 6 [30]
**Rnd 6:** 2 sc, 1 inc, (4 sc, 1 inc) × 5, 2 sc [36]
**Rnd 7:** (5 sc, 1 inc) × 6 [42]
**Rnd 8:** 3 sc, 1 inc, (6 sc, 1 inc) × 5, 3 sc [48]
**Rnd 9:** 48 sc
**Rnd 10:** (5 sc, 1 inc) × 8 [56]
**Rnds 11–22:** 56 sc (12 rounds)
Insert the eyes between **rounds 17** and **18**, with 7 sc visible apart from each other.
**Rnd 23:** (5 sc, 1 dec) × 8 [48]
**Rnd 24:** 2 sc, 1 dec, (4 sc, 1 dec) × 7, 2 sc [40]
**Rnd 25:** 1 sc, 1 dec, (2 sc, 1 dec) × 9, 1 sc [30]
**Rnd 26:** (1 sc, 1 dec) × 10 [20]
Stuff the Head until round 26. You should not stuff from round 27 on.
**Rnd 27:** Blo 20 sc
**Rnds 28–35:** 20 sc (8 rounds)
**Rnd 36:** 10 dec [10]
Fasten off with an inverted magic ring.
Push the neck inward (from round 27 to 36) with the help of the hook handle.
For more instructions, see page 167.

### EARS (MAKE 2)

With **Shell**, make a magic ring.
**Rnd 1:** In ring: 1 sc, 4 hdc, 1 sc
Finish off and leave a long tail to sew.

### NOSE

With **Shell**.
Embroider the Nose between **rounds 18** and **19**, leaving **2 sc** away from the eyes. Pass the thread horizontally **2 times** at a distance of **3 sc**. Then, pass the same thread several times vertically and fasten off.

### EYEBROWS (MAKE 2)

Using the **Brown** embroidery thread, make the Eyebrows with their outer corner 1 round above the eyes and the inner corner 2 rounds above the eyes, with a width of 4 sc.

### LEFT LEG

With **Shell**.

We will work on both sides of the chains. Start with 5 chains and from the second chain from the hook make:

**Rnd 1:** 1 inc, 2 sc, in the last chain 4 sc, continue on the other side of the chains 2 sc, 1 inc [12]

**Rnd 2:** 2 inc, 2 sc, 4 inc, 2 sc, 2 inc [20]

**Rnd 3:** 20 BPsc

**Rnd 4:** 20 sc

**Rnd 5:** 6 sc, 4 dec, 6 sc [16]

**Rnd 6:** 5 sc, 3 dec, 5 sc [13]

**Rnds 7–13:** 13 sc (7 rounds)

Stuff the Leg and fasten off.

If you want your amigurumi to have flat feet to stand, make sure that you don't stuff it too much and leave it concave.

### RIGHT LEG AND BODY

Repeat rounds 1 to 13 of the Left Leg.

Make **4 more sc** and **2 chains** to get to the side of the Leg. Be sure that both feet are facing forward at the junction of the Legs.

**Rnd 14:** 13 sc, 2 sc on the chain, 13 sc, 2 sc on the chain [30]

**Rnds 15–18:** 30 sc (4 rounds)

**Rnd 19:** (13 sc, 1 dec) × 2 [28]

**Rnd 20:** 28 sc

**Rnd 21:** 6 sc, 1 dec, 12 sc, 1 dec, 6 sc [26]

**Rnd 22:** (11 sc, 1 dec) × 2 [24]

**Rnds 23–24:** 24 sc (2 rounds)

**Rnd 25:** 2 sc, 1 dec, (4 sc, 1 dec) × 3, 2 sc [20]
**Rnd 26:** (8 sc, 1 dec) × 2 [18]
**Rnds 27–33:** 18 sc (7 rounds)
**Rnd 34:** 9 dec [9]
Stuff the Body and leave a long tail.

## ARMS (MAKE 2)

With **Shell**.
**Rnd 1:** 6 sc in magic ring
**Rnd 2:** (2 sc, 1 inc) × 2 [8]
**Rnds 3–8:** 8 sc (6 rounds)
Stuff half of the Arms (until round 5).
Pinch Arm opening closed and crochet together with 4 sc. Leave a long tail.

## HAIR (PART I)

With **Black Coffee**.
**Rnd 1:** 6 sc in magic ring
**Rnd 2:** 6 inc [12]
**Rnd 3:** (1 sc, 1 inc) × 6 [18]
**Rnd 4:** 1 sc, 1 inc, (2 sc, 1 inc) × 5, 1 sc [24]
**Rnd 5:** (3 sc, 1 inc) × 6 [30]
**Rnd 6:** 2 sc, 1 inc, (4 sc, 1 inc) × 5, 2 sc [36]
**Rnd 7:** (5 sc, 1 inc) × 6 [42]
**Rnd 8:** 3 sc, 1 inc, (6 sc, 1 inc) × 5, 3 sc [48]
**Rnd 9:** 48 sc
**Rnd 10:** (5 sc, 1 inc) × 8 [56]
Now we will work in rows until the end of the Hair. Make 1 chain and turn the piece.
**Rows 11–20:** 36 sc, 1 chain and turn (10 rows)
**Row 21:** 1 dec, 32 sc, 1 dec, 1 chain and turn [34]
**Row 22:** 1 dec, 30 sc, 1 dec, 1 chain and turn [32]
Fasten off.

## HAIR (PART II)

With **Black Coffee**.
Position the Hair (Part I) upside down. Connect the yarn again in the first loop on right side of the front of the Hair.
Work 12 chains, and from the third chain from the hook make 10 hdc. Close the strand of Hair with 1 sl st in the following st. Make 1 sl st and restart the sequence.
Continue to make 8 strands of Hair and leave the 3 remaining stitches unworked. Fasten off the yarn.

## SKIRT

With **Forest Green**.
Start with 28 chains and close them in a ring with 1 sc. This is the first st of the round.
**Rnds 1–2:** 28 sc (2 rounds)
**Rnd 3:** (1 sl st, 5 chains and from the second chain from the hook 1 sc, 2 hdc, 1 dc. Skip 2 sc and 1 sl st in the following) × 7
**Note:** You will have 7 small triangles
**Rnd 4:** (1 sl st, 2 hdc, 2 sc, 2 chains, 1 sl st in the second chain from the hook, 2 sc, 2 hdc, 1 sl st) × 7
Fasten off.

## STRAP

With **Root Beer**.
Make 30 chains and from the second chain from the hook make (1 sl st, 1 chain) × 29.

### ASSEMBLY

Attach the Skirt to the Body.
Sew the Arms between rounds 25 and 26 on the side of the Body.
Using a tapestry needle attach the Head to the Body, pass the remaining tail of the Head and the remaining tail of the Body to the middle of the magic ring that started the Head.
Pull the two ends in order to adjust the Head to the Body, tie a knot and cut the tails. This way, the Head will be articulated.
Sew the Ears between rounds 16 and 18 (same line as the eyes), 3 sc apart from the eyes.
Make the details on the outer corner of the eyes with **Snow White**. See page 164.
If you want the eyes to be indented, see instructions on page 164.
Sew the Strap on the side of the Skirt, passing from the front of the Body to the back.
Tip: I advise pinning every strand of Hair before applying glue. Just a drop of glue in each strand of Hair should be enough to fix it.
Place the Hair on the Head, arranging the pompadour in a way that every curl is leaning to the left side of the doll's Head.
Make sure that the 8th strand of Hair is covering the 3 unworked stitches from Part II of the Hair.

# Snake

## YARN

Fingering weight (#1 super fine) yarn, shown in Scheepjes *Catona* (100% mercerized cotton, 174 yd. / 125 m per 1.75 oz. / 50 g ball)

**HEAD/BODY**

525 Fir

110 Jet Black

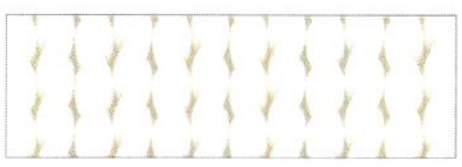

105 Bridal White

## FINISHED MEASUREMENTS

**LENGTH:** 15 in. / 38 cm

## HOOK

- US B-1 / 2.0 mm crochet hook

## NOTIONS

- Polyester stuffing
- Tapestry needle
- Removable stitch markers
- Pointy tweezers
- Craft wire or flexible plastic skeleton/armature for toys
- Pair of 12 mm safety eyes

## GAUGE

*Gauge is not critical for this project. Ensure your stitches are tight so the stuffing won't show through.*

For more information on how to make the Snake, including tips, step-by-step pictures, and videos, scan this QR code!

## HEAD/BODY

With **Fir**.

We will work on both sides of the chains. Start with 5 chains, and from the second chain from the hook, work as follows:

**Rnd 1:** 1 inc, 2 sc, in the last chain 4 sc, continue on the other side of the chains 2 sc, 1 inc [12]

**Rnd 2:** 1 inc, 4 sc, 2 inc, 4 sc, 1 inc [16]

**Rnd 3:** 16 sc

**Rnd 4:** 2 inc, 4 sc, 4 inc, 4 sc, 2 inc [24]

**Rnd 5:** 1 sc, 1 inc, 8 sc, (1 sc, 1 inc) × 2, 9 sc, 1 inc [28]

**Rnd 6:** 1 sc, (2 sc, 1 inc) × 4, 15 [32]

**Rnds 7–11:** 32 (5 rounds)

**Rnd 12:** (2 sc, 1 dec) × 4, 16 sc [28]

Insert the eyes between rounds 7 and 8, 10 sc apart from each other (6 visible stitches). The first eye should be after the third stitch of the round.

**Rnd 13:** 1 sc, (1 sc, 1 dec) × 4, 15 sc [24]

**Rnd 14:** 2 sc, 1 dec, (4 sc, 1 dec) × 3, 2 sc [20]

**Rnds 15–16:** 20 sc (2 rounds)

**Rnd 17:** 4 dec, 3 sc, 6 inc, 3 sc [22]

**Rnd 18:** 22 sc

**Rnd 19:** 3 dec, 6 sc, 3 inc, 7 sc [22]

**Rnd 20:** 22 sc

**Rnd 21:** 3 dec, 5 sc, 2 inc, 7 sc, 1 dec [20]

**Rnd 22:** 20 sc

**Rnd 23:** 1 dec, 8 sc, 2 inc, 6 sc, 1 dec [20]

Make 10 sc to get to the back of the Snake. The following stitch will be the first of the round from now on. **Note:** The color changes are on the back of the Snake. You can make more or less sc, according to your crochet tension, to get to this point. Stuff the Head firmly and continue adding stuffing as you crochet. If you want the Snake to be articulated, insert craft wire or the skeleton at this stage, and continue crocheting and stuffing as you go.

**Rnd 24:** Change to **Jet Black**. 20 sc

**Rnds 25–26:** Change to **Bridal White**. 20 sc (2 rounds)

**Rnd 27:** Change to **Jet Black**. 20 sc

**Rnds 28–30:** Change to **Fir**. 20 sc (3 rounds)

**Rnd 31:** (1 dec, 8 sc) × 2 [18]

**Rnd 32:** Change to **Jet Black**. 18 sc

**Rnds 33–34:** Change to **Bridal White**. 18 sc (2 rounds)

**Rnd 35:** Change to **Jet Black**. 18 sc

**Rnds 36–39:** Change to **Fir**. 18 sc (4 rounds)

**Rnd 40:** Change to **Jet Black**. 18 sc

**Rnds 41–42:** Change to **Bridal White**. 18 sc (2 rounds)

**Rnd 43:** Change to **Jet Black**. 18 sc

**Rnds 44–47:** Change to **Fir**. 18 sc (4 rounds)

**Rnd 48:** Change to **Jet Black**. 18 sc

**Rnds 49–50:** Change to **Bridal White**. 18 sc (2 rounds)

**Rnd 51:** Change to **Jet Black**. 18 sc

**Rnds 52–55:** Change to **Fir**. 18 sc (4 rounds)

**Rnd 56:** Change to **Jet Black**. 18 sc

**Rnds 57–58:** Change to **Bridal White**. 18 sc (2 rounds)

**Rnd 59:** Change to **Jet Black**. 18 sc

**Rnds 60–63:** Change to **Fir**. 18 sc (4 rounds)

**Rnd 64:** Change to **Jet Black**. (4 sc, 1 dec) × 3 [15]

**Rnds 65–66:** Change to **Bridal White**. 15 sc (2 rounds)

**Rnd 67:** Change to **Jet Black**. 15 sc

**Rnds 68–71:** Change to **Fir**. 15 sc (4 rounds)

**Rnd 72:** Change to **Jet Black**. (4 sc, 1 dec) × 3 [15]

**Rnds 73–74:** Change to **Bridal White**. 15 sc (2 rounds)

**Rnd 75:** Change to **Jet Black**. 15 sc

**Rnds 76–79:** Change to **Fir**. 15 sc (4 rounds)
**Rnd 80:** Change to **Jet Black**. (3 sc, 1 dec) × 3 [12]
**Rnds 81–82:** Change to **Bridal White**. 12 sc (2 rounds)
**Rnd 83:** Change to **Jet Black**. 12 sc
**Rnds 84–87:** Change to **Fir**. 12 sc (4 rounds)
**Rnd 88:** Change to **Jet Black**. (2 sc, 1 dec) × 3 [9]
**Rnds 89–90:** Change to **Bridal White**. 9 sc (2 rounds)
**Rnd 91:** Change to **Jet Black**. 9 sc
Fasten off both the **Jet Black** and **Bridal White** yarns. If you are using any material to make the snake **movable**, cut the craft wire at round 93. This will make the final steps easier and help you close the amigurumi neatly.
**Rnds 92–94:** Change to **Fir**. 9 sc (3 rounds)
**Rnd 95:** (1 sc, 1 dec) × 3 [6]
Close it with an inverted magic ring and fasten off.
If you inserted the craft wire earlier, now you can gently shape the amigurumi with your hands, adjusting the curves until you achieve the desired twisted form.

# The Story of Noah and the Ark

Genesis 6–8

**The story of Noah is one of destruction and redemption. Noah was a good man who walked with God, as did his wife and three sons. But the wickedness and violence of mankind was running rampant. So God decided to wipe out mankind altogether with a great flood that covered the earth, but he would spare Noah, giving him instructions to build an ark. He then instructed Noah:**

> But with thee will I establish my covenant; and thou shalt come into the ark, thou, and thy sons, and thy wife, and thy sons' wives with thee.[18] And of every living thing of all flesh, two of every sort shalt thou bring into the ark, to keep them alive with thee; they shall be male and female.[19] Of fowls after their kind, and of cattle after their kind, of every creeping thing of the earth after his kind, two of every sort shall come unto thee, to keep them alive.[20] And take thou unto thee of all food that is eaten, and thou shalt gather it to thee; and it shall be for food for thee, and for them.[21] Thus did Noah; according to all that God commanded him, so did he.[22]

**—Genesis 6:18–22**

God then made it rain for forty days and forty nights; the flood waters prevailed for a hundred and fifty days, until every creature that drew breath on the earth died. But God remembered Noah, sending a wind to carry the ark to the top of Mount Ararat until the waters receded. Noah sent out doves to see if the waters had gone; when one brought back an olive branch, he knew it was safe to return.

Here, our Noah is leading an Elephant and Giraffe to the ark, preserving two of the most fantastic beasts of God's creation.

# Noah

## YARN

Fingering weight (#1 super fine) yarn, shown in Scheepjes *Catona*, (100% mercerized cotton, 174 yd. / 125 m per 1.75 oz. / 50 g ball)

**SKIN**

255 Shell

**SHOES**

162 Black Coffee

**HAIR**

105 Bridal White

**EYE DETAIL**

106 Snow White

Fingering weight (#1 super fine) yarn, shown in Hobbii *Friends Cotton 8/4* (100% cotton, 174 yd. / 160 m per 1.75 oz. / 50 g ball)

**OUTFIT**

108 Pistachio

**BELT**

13 Ochre

**VEST**

82 Prussian Blue

## FINISHED MEASUREMENTS

**HEIGHT:** 5.5 in. / 14 cm
**WIDTH:** 3.15 in. / 8 cm

## HOOK

- US B-1 / 2.0 mm crochet hook for the Body
- US C-2 / 2.5 mm crochet hook for the Hair, Beard, and Mustache

***Note:*** *Everything is worked with US B-1 / 2.0 mm crochet hook except for the Hair, Beard, and Mustache.*

## NOTIONS

- Pair of 13 mm safety eyes
- Polyester stuffing
- Tapestry needle
- Removable stitch markers
- Sewing pins
- Pointy tweezers
- Craft glue
- Craft wire

## GAUGE

*Gauge is not critical for this project. Ensure your stitches are tight so the stuffing won't show through.*

For more information on how to make Noah, including tips, step-by-step pictures, and videos, scan this QR code!

## HEAD

With **Shell**.
**Rnd 1:** 6 sc in magic ring
**Rnd 2:** 6 inc [12]
**Rnd 3:** (1 sc, 1 inc) × 6 [18]
**Rnd 4:** 1 sc, 1 inc, (2 sc, 1 inc) × 5, 1 sc [24]
**Rnd 5:** (3 sc, 1 inc) × 6 [30]
**Rnd 6:** 2 sc, 1 inc, (4 sc, 1 inc) × 5, 2 sc [36]
**Rnd 7:** (5 sc, 1 inc) × 6 [42]
**Rnd 8:** 3 sc, 1 inc, (6 sc, 1 inc) × 5, 3 sc [48]
**Rnd 9:** 48 sc
**Rnd 10:** (5 sc, 1 inc) × 8 [56]
**Rnds 11–22:** 56 sc (12 rounds)
Insert the eyes between rounds 17 and 18, with 7 sc visible apart from each other.
**Rnd 23:** (5 sc, 1 dec) × 8 [48]
**Rnd 24:** 2 sc, 1 dec, (4 sc, 1 dec) × 7, 2 sc [40]
**Rnd 25:** 1 sc, 1 dec, (2 sc, 1 dec) × 9, 1 sc [30]
**Rnd 26:** (1 sc, 1 dec) × 10 [20]
Stuff the Head until round 26. You should not stuff from round 27 on.
**Rnd 27:** Blo 20 sc
**Rnds 28–35:** 20 sc (8 rounds)
**Rnd 36:** 10 dec [10]
Fasten off with an inverted magic ring.
Push the neck inward (from round 27 to 36) with the help of the hook handle.
For more instructions, see page 167.

## EARS (MAKE 2)

With **Shell**, make a magic ring.
**Rnd 1:** In ring: 1 sc, 4 hdc, 1 sc.
Finish off and leave a long tail.

## NOSE

With **Shell**.
**Rnd 1:** 6 sc in magic ring
**Rnd 2:** (2 sc, 1 inc) × 2 [8]
Finish off and leave a long tail.

## EYEBROWS (MAKE 2)

With **Bridal White**, make 5 chains and cut the yarn, leaving a long tail to attach it to Head. The Eyebrows should be placed with their outer corner 1 round above the eyes and the inner corner 2 rounds above the eyes, with a width of 4 sc.
To finish off, pass both ends through the Head making them leave on the same gap. Then, tie a knot with them and push this knot inside the Head to hide it.

## ROBE

With **Pistachio**, make 35 chains and close them into a ring with 1 sc. This will be the first stitch of the round.
**Rnds 1–6:** 35 sc (6 rounds)
**Rnd 7:** (5 sc, 1 dec) × 5 [30]
**Rnd 8:** 30 sc
**Rnd 9:** (13 sc, 1 dec) × 2 [28]
**Rnd 10:** 28 sc
Don't fasten off, yarn is used to continue working the Body.

## LEFT LEG

With **Black Coffee**.
We will work on both sides of the chains. Start with 5 chains and from the second chain from the hook make:
**Rnd 1:** 1 inc, 2 sc, in the last chain 4 sc, continue on the other side of the chains 2 sc, 1 inc [12]
**Rnd 2:** 2 inc, 2 sc, 4 inc, 2 sc, 2 inc [20]
**Rnd 3:** 20 BPsc
**Rnd 4:** 20 sc
**Rnd 5:** Change to **Shell**. Blo 20 sl st
**Rnd 6:** Insert the hook below both loops of the slip stitch. 20 sc
**Rnd 7:** 6 sc, 4 dec, 6 sc [16]
**Rnd 8:** 5 sc, 3 dec, 5 sc [13]
**Rnds 9–13:** 13 sc (5 rounds)
**Rnds 14–15:** Change to **Bridal White**. 13 sc (2 rounds)
Stuff the Leg and fasten off.
If you want your amigurumi to have flat feet to stand, make sure that you don't stuff it too much and leave it concave.

## RIGHT LEG

Repeat rounds 1 to 15 of the Left Leg.
Make **4 more sc** and **2 chains** to get to the side of the Leg.

## SANDALS

With **Black Coffee**.
Attach the yarn to the 5th loop created by round 5. Make 7 chains, skip 9 loops, and attach the chains with 1 sl st. Fasten off.
Make Sandals for both feet before continuing with the Body.

### BODY

With **Bridal White**, continue the Body by joining both Legs. Be sure that both feet are facing forward at the junction of the Legs. Stuff the Body as you crochet.

**Rnd 16:** 13 sc, 2 sc on the chain, 13 sc, 2 sc on the chain [30]
**Rnds 17–20:** 30 sc (4 rounds)
**Rnd 21:** (13 sc, 1 dec) × 2 [28]
Fasten off **Bridal White**. Place the Robe on the Body. Crochet both pieces together with **Pistachio**.
**Rnd 22:** 28 sc (joining the Body and the Robe)
**Rnd 23:** 28 sc
**Rnd 24:** 6 sc, 1 dec, 12 sc, 1 dec, 6 sc [26]
**Rnd 25:** 26 sc
**Rnd 26:** (11 sc, 1 dec) × 2 [24]
**Rnds 27–28:** 24 sc (2 rounds)
**Rnd 29:** Flo 24 sl st
Fasten off **Pistachio**.
Using the back loops of round 29, attach **Shell** and work:
**Rnd 29:** 24 sc
**Rnd 30:** 2 sc, 1 dec, (4 sc, 1 dec) × 3, 2 sc [20]
**Rnd 31:** (8 sc, 1 dec) × 2 [18]
**Rnds 32–38:** 18 sc (7 rounds)
**Rnd 39:** 9 dec [9]
Stuff the Body, fasten off, and leave a long tail to attach the Body and the Head.

### ARMS (MAKE 2)

With **Shell**.
**Rnd 1:** 6 sc in magic ring
**Rnd 2:** (2 sc, 1 inc) × 2 [8]
**Rnds 3–7:** 8 sc (5 rounds)
**Rnd 8:** (3 sc, 1 inc) × 2 [10]

Slightly stuff half of the Arms (until round 4).
Fasten off.

## SLEEVES (MAKE 2)

With **Pistachio**.
Make 14 chains and close it with 1 sc. This will be the first st of the round:
**Rnds 1–4:** 14 sc (4 rounds)
**Rnd 5:** (5 sc, 1 dec) × 2 [12]
**Rnd 6:** 12 sc
**Rnd 7:** (4 sc, 1 dec) × 2 [10]
**Rnd 8:** 10 sc
Put the Arms inside the Sleeves. Crochet both pieces together:
**Rnd 9:** 10 sc (joining both pieces)
**Rnd 10:** 10 sc
Pinch the Arm opening closed and crochet together with 5 sc. Leave a long tail.

## HAIR

With **Bridal White** and US C-2 / 2.5 mm hook make an oval piece from the foundation chain, by working on both sides of the chains.
Make 12 chains, and from the second chain from the hook make:
1 inc, 9 sc, 4 sc in the last one, 9 sc, 1 inc [26]
Work around the 26 st and make 1 strand of Hair in each of them.
Make 27 chains, and from the third chain from the hook make 25 hdc. Close the strand of Hair with 1 sl st in the following st and restart the sequence.
You will have 26 strands of Hair.

## BEARD

With **Bridal White** and US C-2 / 2.5 mm hook, make 30 chains and from the second chain from the hook:
**Row 1:** 29 sl st, chain and turn
**Row 2:** 5 sl st, 1 incT dc, 1 inc dc, 5 dc, 5 dtr, 5 dc, 1 inc dc, 1 incT dc, 5 sl st
Leave a long tail.

### MUSTACHE

With **Bridal White** and US C-2 / 2.5 mm hook, make 12 chains, and from the second chain from the hook:

**Row 1:** 11 sl st, chain and turn

**Row 2:** 1 sl st, 1 sc, 1 hdc, 1 inc dr, 1 inc dtr, 1 sl st

Leave a long tail.

### VEST

With **Prussian Blue**, make 23 chains and from the second chain from the hook:

**Row 1:** 22 sc, chain and turn

**Row 2:** 3 sc, 6 chains and skip 4 sc, 8 sc, 6 chains and skip 4 sc, 3 sc, chain and turn [26]

**Rows 3–5:** 26 sc, chain and turn (3 rows)

**Row 6:** 12 sc, 2 inc, 12 sc, chain and turn [28]

**Rows 7–8:** 28 sc, chain and turn (2 rows)

**Row 9:** 7 sc, 1 inc, 12 sc, 1 inc, 7 sc, chain and turn [30]

**Rows 10–11:** 30 sc, chain and turn (2 rows)

**Row 12:** 10 sc, 1 inc, 8 sc, 1 inc, 10 sc, chain and turn [32]

**Row 13:** 32 sc

Now crochet around the Vest.

On one side, make 12 sc and 3 hdc together in the last st.

On the top part of the Vest (the collar), crochet 22 hd.

On the other side of the Vest, make 3 hdc together and 12 sc.

Fasten off.

## BELT

With **Ochre**.

Make 52 chains and from the second chain from the hook make 51 sl st.

Fasten off.

## STAFF

Cut the craft wire to measure around 4 in. / 10 cm.

With **Black Coffee**, place a drop of glue at the tip of the Staff to fix it, and continue wrapping the yarn all over the wire to cover it. Glue to the opposite end of the Staff and cut the yarn.

## ASSEMBLY

Using a tapestry needle to attach the Head to the Body, pass the remaining tail of the Head and the remaining tail of the Body to the middle of the magic ring that started the Head.

Pull the two ends in order to adjust the Head to the Body, tie a knot and cut the tails. This way, the Head will be articulated.

Sew the Nose between rounds 17 and 18, between the eyes, leaving 3 sc distance from the Nose to the eyes.

Sew the Arms between rounds 25 and 26, on the side of the Body, with 9 sc distant in the front part of the Body.

Place the Vest on the doll and add the Belt on top of it, knotting the ends.

Place the Beard in a way that the Sideburns start from round 15 to 18, and the flat bottom part is 3 rounds below the eyes.

Sew the Mustache just below the Nose.

Sew the Ears between rounds 16 and 18 (same line as the eyes), 3 sc apart from the eyes.

Make the details on the outer corner of the eyes with **Snow White**, see page 164.

If you want the eyes to be indented, see instructions on page 164.

**Note:** I advise pinning every strand of Hair before applying glue. Just a drop of glue in each strand of Hair should be enough to fix it.

Place the Hair on the Head of your amigurumi. The oval piece, which is the foundation of the Hair, should be on the top of the Head.

Split the Hair into 13 strands for each side. Leave 4 strands of Hair loose in front of the Ears (8 strands in total).

Pin the remaining strands of Hair around the Head, behind the Ears. You will have 18 strands of Hair.

Make sure the remaining strands are evenly divided, 4 on each side, and gently swept backward.

# Elephant

## YARN

Fingering weight (#1 super fine) yarn, shown in Scheepjes *Catona* (100% mercerized cotton, 174 yd. / 125 m per 1.75 oz. / 50 g ball)

**BODY**

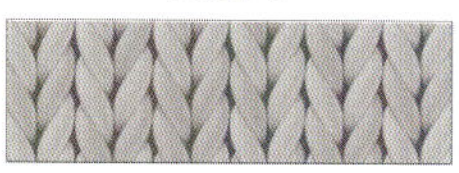

074 Mercury

**INNER EARS**

408 Old Rose

**PAW DETAILS**

106 Snow White

Lace yarn (#0 lace) in black color. Any standard black embroidery thread can be used for the eyebrows.

## FINISHED MEASUREMENTS

**HEIGHT:** 5.9 in. / 15 cm
**WIDTH:** 6.7 in. / 17 cm

## HOOK

- US B-1 / 2.0 mm crochet hook

## NOTIONS

- Pair of 14 mm safety eyes
- Polyester stuffing
- Tapestry needle
- Removable stitch markers
- Sewing pins
- Pointy tweezers

## GAUGE

*Gauge is not critical for this project. Ensure your stitches are tight so the stuffing won't show through.*

For more information on how to make the Elephant, including tips, step-by-step pictures, and videos, scan this QR code!

### TRUNK

With **Mercury**.
**Rnd 1:** 6 sc in magic ring
**Rnd 2:** Blo (1 sc, 1 inc) × 3 [9]
**Rnd 3:** 9 sc
**Rnd 4:** (2 sc, 1 inc) × 3 [12]
**Rnds 5–6:** 12 sc (2 rounds)
**Rnd 7:** (3 sc, 1 inc) × 3 [15]
**Rnds 8–10:** 15 sc (3 rounds)
**Rnd 11:** (4 sc, 1 inc) × 3 [18]
**Rnds 12–14:** 18 sc (3 rounds)
**Rnd 15:** (5 sc, 1 inc) × 3 [21]
**Rnds 16–18:** 21 sc (3 rounds)
**Rnd 19:** (6 sc, 1 inc) × 3 [24]
**Rnds 20–24:** 24 sc (5 rounds)
Fasten off.

### LEGS (MAKE 4)

With **Mercury**.
**Rnd 1:** 8 sc in magic ring
**Rnd 2:** 8 inc [16]
**Rnd 3:** (1 sc, 1 inc) × 8 [24]
**Rnd 4:** 24 BPsc
**Rnds 5–11:** 24 sc (7 rounds)
Fasten off.

### BELLY BOTTOM AND BODY

With **Mercury**.
**Rnd 1:** 8 sc in magic ring
**Rnd 2:** 8 inc [16]
**Rnd 3:** (1 sc, 1 inc) × 8 [24]
**Rnd 4:** (3 sc, 1 inc) × 6 [30]
**Rnd 5:** 2 sc, 1 inc, (4 sc, 1 inc) × 5, 2 sc [36]
Do not fasten off.

Join the Legs to the Belly Bottom:
**Rnd 12:** 5 sc joining the first Leg, 7 sc in the Belly Bottom, 5 sc joining the second Leg, 1 sc in the Belly Bottom, 5 sc joining the third Leg, 7 sc in the Belly Bottom, 5 sc joining the fourth Leg, 1 sc in the Belly Bottom [92] *
*Count the stitches around the crochet piece. Continue working to make the rest of the Body.
**Rnd 13:** (22 sc, 1 inc) × 4 [96]
**Rnds 14–23:** 96 sc (10 rounds)
**Rnd 24:** 5 sc, 1 dec, (10 sc, 1 dec) × 7, 5 sc [88]
**Rnd 25:** (9 sc, 1 dec) × 8 [80]
**Rnd 26:** 80 sc
**Rnd 27:** 4 sc, 1 dec, (8 sc, 1 dec) × 7, 4 sc [72]
**Rnds 28–29:** 72 sc (2 rounds)
**Rnd 30:** 24 sc, make 14 chains and skip 24 sc, 24 sc
Observe that you should have 48 sc in the back of the Elephant and 24 sc in the front (separated by the 14 chains in the middle).
We will work on each part separately, using both sides of the chains to close the Back of the Body and to crochet the neck and the Head.

### BACK

**Rnd 31:** (29 sc, 1 dec) × 2 [60]
**Rnd 32:** 4 sc, 1 dec, (8 sc, 1 dec) × 5, 4 sc [54]

**Rnd 33:** (7 sc, 1 dec) × 6 [48]
**Rnd 34:** 2 sc, 1 dec, (4 sc, 1 dec) × 7, 2 sc [40]
**Rnd 35:** (3 sc, 1 dec) × 8 [32]
**Rnd 36:** 1 sc, 1 dec, (2 sc, 1 dec) × 7, 1 sc [24]
**Rnd 37:** (1 sc, 1 dec) × 8 [16]
**Rnd 38:** 8 dec (8)
Close it with an inverted magic ring.
Stuff the Body, especially the Back part, using the hole from the Head that is still open. Make sure that it is firm, as we will continue crocheting the Head. From now on, continue stuffing as you crochet.

## HEAD

Insert the hook in the first stitch right next to the chains (it should be the 25th stitch of round 30 of the Body). Crochet in every loop of the chains and the sc that you skipped in round 30 of the Body.
**Rnd 31:** (17 sc, 1 dec) × 2 [36]
**Rnd 32:** (1 sc, 1 inc) × 18 [54]
**Rnd 33:** 4 sc, 1 inc, (8 sc, 1 inc) × 5, 4 sc [60]
**Rnd 34:** (9 sc, 1 inc) × 6 [66]
**Rnd 35:** 5 sc, 1 inc, (10 sc, 1 inc) × 5, 5 sc [72]
**Rnd 36:** (11 sc, 1 inc) × 6 [78]
**Rnds 37–40:** 78 sc (4 rounds)
We will attach the Trunk on the following round. The important thing is that you have the Trunk attached to the front of the face, and the total number of stitches in the round is the same.

**Row 12:** 8 sc, chain and turn
**Row 13:** 1 dec, 6 sc, chain and turn [7]
**Row 14:** 7 sc, chain and turn
**Row 15:** 1 dec, 5 sc, chain and turn [6]
**Row 16:** 6 sc, chain and turn
**Row 17:** 1 dec, 4 sc, chain and turn [5]
**Row 18:** 5 sc

We will now work making sc around the piece.

After row 18, make 1 chain, and continue with 11 sc, 32 sc in the round part, 11 sc, 1 chain, 1 dec, 1 sc, 1 dec.

Fasten off.

## RIGHT EAR (PART II)

With **Mercury**.

Repeat the instructions above for Part I but do not fasten off.

Place the **Old Rose** piece together with the **Mercury** one. Crochet both pieces together using single crochet (sc).

Leave a long tail for sewing.

## EYEBROWS (MAKE 2)

Using the **Black** embroidery thread, make the Eyebrows with their outer corner 1 round above the eyes and the inner corner 2 rounds above the eyes, with a width of 4 sc.

## TAIL

With **Mercury**.

Make 18 chains, and from the third chain from the hook, make 16 hdc.

Leave a long tail for sewing.

## ASSEMBLY

Sew the Ears on the sides of the Head, 5 sc apart from the eyes. Pin the Ears to make sure they are in the right place and at the same height.

If you want the eyes to be indented, see instructions on page 164.

Make the details on the outer corner of the eyes with **Snow White**, see page 164.

Make the details on the paws with **Snow White**. Make 3 toes on each paw, with 3 sc apart from each other. Pass the yarn vertically twice between rounds 5 and 7. Then, pass it twice on the right and left sides of these first lines, between rounds 5 and 6.

Sew the Tail in the back of the Elephant, between rounds 32 and 33.

Fasten off.

# Giraffe

**FINISHED MEASUREMENTS**
**HEIGHT:** 8.25 in. / 21 cm
**WIDTH:** 2.4 in. / 6 cm

**HOOK**
- US B-1 / 2.0 mm crochet hook

**NOTIONS**
- Pair of 12 mm safety eyes
- Polyester stuffing
- Tapestry needle
- Removable stitch markers
- Sewing pins
- Pointy tweezers

**GAUGE**
*Gauge is not critical for this project. Ensure your stitches are tight so the stuffing won't show through.*

For more information on how to make the Giraffe, including tips, step-by-step pictures, and videos, scan this QR code!

## YARN

Fingering weight (#1 super fine) yarn, shown in Scheepjes *Catona* (100% mercerized cotton, 174 yd. / 125 m per 1.75 oz. / 50 g ball)

**BODY/EARS**

208 Yellow Gold

**PAW**

162 Black Coffee

**MUZZLE**

505 Linen

Lace yarn (#0 lace) in brown color. Any standard brown embroidery thread can be used for the eyebrows.

## LEGS (MAKE 4)

With **Black Coffee**.
**Rnd 1:** 8 sc in magic ring
**Rnd 2:** 8 inc [16]
**Rnd 3:** (3 sc, 1 inc) × 4 [20]
**Rnd 4:** 20 BPsc
**Rnd 5:** 20 sc
**Rnd 6:** Change to **Yellow Gold**. 20 sc
**Rnds 7–11:** 20 sc (5 rounds)
Fasten off.

## BELLY BOTTOM AND BODY

With **Yellow Gold**. We will work around the foundation chains. Start with 9 chains and in the second chain from the hook, make:
**Rnd 1:** 1 inc, 6 sc, 4 sc in the last chain, 6 sc, 1 inc [20]
**Rnd 2:** 2 inc, 6 sc, 4 inc, 6 sc, 2 inc [28]
**Rnd 3:** (1 sc, 1 inc) × 2, 6 sc, (1 sc, 1 inc) × 4, 6 sc, (1 sc, 1 inc) × 2 [36]
Do not fasten off.

Join the Legs to the Belly Bottom:
Place the Belly Bottom with the inverted side of the magic ring facing up.
**Rnd 12:** 1 sc in the Belly Bottom, 5 sc joining the first Leg, 6 sc in the Belly Bottom, 5 sc joining the second Leg, 2 sc in the Belly Bottom, 5 sc joining the third Leg, 6 sc in the Belly Bottom, 5 sc joining the fourth Leg, 1 sc in the Belly Bottom [76] *
*Count the stitches around the crochet piece.

**Rnds 13–23:** 76 sc (11 rounds)
**Rnd 24:** (17 sc, 1 dec) × 4 [72]
**Rnd 25:** 72 sc
**Rnd 26:** 22 sc, make 12 chains and skip 28 sc, 22 sc

Observe that you should have 44 sc in the back of the Giraffe and 28 sc in the front.

We will work on each part separately, using both sides of the chains to close the Back and to crochet the Neck.

## BACK

**Rnd 27:** 22 sc, 12 sc in one side of the chains, 22 sc [56]
**Rnd 28:** (5 sc, 1 dec) × 8 [48]
**Rnd 29:** 2 sc, 1 dec, (4 sc, 1 dec) × 7, 2 sc [40]
**Rnd 30:** (3 sc, 1 dec) × 8 [32]
**Rnd 31:** 1 sc, 1 dec, (2 sc, 1 dec) × 7, 1 sc [24]
**Rnd 32:** (1 sc, 1 dec) × 8 [16]
**Rnd 33:** 8 dec [8]

Close it with an inverted magic ring.

Stuff the Body of the Giraffe, especially the Back part, using the hole from the Neck that is still open. Make sure that it is firm, as we will continue crocheting the Neck. From now on, continue stuffing as you crochet.

## NECK AND HEAD

Insert the hook in the loops of the other side of the chains, as this will be the back of the Neck. Crochet in every loop of the chains and the sc that you skipped in round 26 of the Body.

**Rnd 27:** 40 sc
**Rnd 28:** (3 sc, 1 dec) × 8 [32]
**Rnds 29–32:** 32 sc (4 rounds)
**Rnd 33:** 3 sc, 1 dec, (6 sc, 1 dec) × 3, 3 sc [28]
**Rnds 34–37:** 28 sc (4 rounds)
**Rnd 38:** (5 sc, 1 dec) × 4 [24]
**Rnds 39–42:** 24 sc (4 rounds)
**Rnd 43:** 24 FPsc
**Rnd 44:** (1 sc, 1 inc) × 12 [36]
**Rnd 45:** 1 sc, 1 inc, (2 sc, 1 inc) × 11, 1 sc [48]
**Rnd 46:** 48 sc
**Rnd 47:** (7 sc, 1 inc) × 6 [54]
**Rnds 48–60:** 54 sc (13 rounds)
Insert the eyes between rounds 54 and 55, with visible 10 sc apart from each other. Stuff the Neck and continue stuffing the Head as you close the amigurumi.
**Rnd 61:** (7 sc, 1 dec) × 6 [48]
**Rnd 62:** 2 sc, 1 dec, (4 sc, 1 dec) × 7, 2 sc [40]
**Rnd 63:** (3 sc, 1 dec) × 8 [32]
**Rnd 64:** 1 sc, 1 dec, (2 sc, 1 dec) × 7, 1 sc [24]
**Rnd 65:** (1 sc, 1 dec) × 8 [16]
**Rnd 66:** 8 dec [8]
Close it with an inverted magic ring and fasten off.

## EARS (MAKE 2)

With **Yellow Gold**.
**Rnd 1:** 6 sc in magic ring
**Rnd 2:** (1 sc, 1 inc) × 3 [9]
**Rnd 3:** (2 sc, 1 inc) × 3 [12]
**Rnd 4:** (3 sc, 1 inc) × 3 [15]
**Rnd 5:** (4 sc, 1 inc) × 3 [18]
**Rnds 6–8:** 18 sc (3 rounds)
Leave a long tail.

## MUZZLE

With **Linen**.
We will work on both sides of the chain. Start with 6 chains and on the second chain from the hook, make:
**Rnd 1:** 1 inc, 3 sc, in the last chain 4 sc, in the other side of the chains 3 sc, 1 inc [14]
**Rnd 2:** 2 inc, 3 sc, 4 inc, 3 sc, 2 inc [22]
**Rnd 3:** (1 sc, 1 inc) × 2, 3 sc, (1 sc, 1 inc) × 4, 3 sc, (1 sc, 1 inc) × 2 [30]
**Rnd 4:** 30 sc
**Rnd 5:** (2 sc, 1 inc) × 2, 3 sc, (2 sc, 1 inc) × 4, 3 sc, (2 sc, 1 inc) × 2 [38]
**Rnds 6–7:** 38 sc (2 rounds)
Leave a long tail.

## EARS (MAKE 2)

With **Black Coffee**.
**Rnd 1:** 6 sc in magic ring
**Rnd 2:** 6 inc [12]
**Rnd 3:** (2 sc, 1 inc) × 4 [16]
**Rnd 4:** 16 sc
**Rnd 5:** 8 dec [8]
Stuff the piece as you crochet.
**Rnd 6:** Change to **Yellow Gold**. 8 sc
**Rnds 7–10:** 8 sc (4 rounds)
Leave a long tail.

### SPOTS (MAKE 8)

With **Black Coffee**.
**Rnd 1:** 6 sc in magic ring
**Rnd 2:** 6 inc [12]
Leave a long tail.

### TAIL

With **Black Coffee**.
**Rnd 1:** 6 sc in magic ring
**Rnd 2:** (1 sc, 1 inc) × 3 [9]
**Rnd 3:** (2 sc, 1 inc) × 3 [12]
**Rnd 4:** (3 sc, 1 inc) × 3 [15]
**Rnd 5:** 15 sc
**Rnd 6:** (3 sc, 1 dec) × 3 [12]
**Rnd 7:** (1 sc, 1 dec) × 4 [8]
Stuff the Tail as you crochet.
**Rnd 8:** Change to **Yellow Gold**. 8 sc
**Rnds 9–20:** 8 sc (12 rounds)
Leave a long tail.

### ASSEMBLY

If you want the eyes to be indented, see page 164.

Sew the Muzzle right below the eyes, between rounds 43 and 53.

Before attaching the Ears, pinch the bottom closed. Pass the tapestry needle from one edge to the other and attach the Ears between rounds 57 and 58, 5 sc apart from the eyes.

With the **Brown** embroidery thread, embroider the eyebrows 2 rounds above the eyes, using the width of 3 sc and 1 sc of height.

Make the details on the outer corner of the eyes with **Snow White**, see page 164.

Sew the Ears on top of the Head, 4 sc apart from each other.

Sew the Spots on the Body, as you like. I recommend pinning the Spots first to find a position that you like.

Sew the Tail on the Back, between rounds 25 and 26.

"And the rainbow shall be in the cloud; and I will look upon it, that I may remember the everlasting covenant between God and every living creature of all flesh that is upon the earth. And God said unto Noah, This is the token of the covenant, which I have established between me and all flesh that is upon the earth."

—Genesis 9:16–17

# Heroes and Judges

# The Stories of Moses

**Exodus 14, 20**

**As a young man, the prophet Moses encountered God within a burning bush in the desert and was commanded to return to Egypt to liberate the Jews from slavery. God then unleashed a series of ten devastating plagues, giving the Jews an opportunity to escape. Moses led the Jews into the wilderness, where this amigurumi illustrates this extraordinary part of the story:**

> But the Egyptians pursued after them, all the horses and chariots of Pharaoh, and his horsemen, and his army, and overtook them encamping by the sea, beside Pihahiroth, before Baalzephon.[9] And when Pharaoh drew nigh, the children of Israel lifted up their eyes, and, behold, the Egyptians marched after them; and they were sore afraid: and the children of Israel cried out unto the Lord.[10] And they said unto Moses, Because there were no graves in Egypt, hast thou taken us away to die in the wilderness? Wherefore hast thou dealt thus with us, to carry us forth out of Egypt?[11] And Moses said unto the people, Fear ye not, stand still, and see the salvation of the Lord, which he will shew to you to day: for the Egyptians whom ye have seen to day, ye shall see them again no more for ever.[13] And Moses stretched out his hand over the sea; and the Lord caused the sea to go back by a strong east wind all that night, and made the sea dry land, and the waters were divided.[21] And the children of Israel went into the midst of the sea upon the dry ground: and the waters were a wall unto them on their right hand, and on their left.[22]

**—Exodus 14:9–11, 13, 21–22**

Moses is also shown with the tablets of the Ten Commandments, the divine laws given to Moses by God on Mount Sinai for the Israelites (Exodus 20).

# Moses

## YARN

Fingering weight (#1 super fine) yarn, shown in Scheepjes *Catona* (100% mercerized cotton, 174 yd. / 125 m per 1.75 oz. / 50 g ball)

**SKIN**
255 Shell

**UNDERWEAR**
105 Bridal White

**SHOES**
157 Root Beer

**HAIR/BEARD**
074 Mercury

**EYE DETAIL**
106 Snow White

**ROBE**
517 Ruby

**ROCK**
393 Charcoal

Fingering weight (#1 super fine) yarn, shown in Hobbii *Tencel Bamboo Fine* (40% Tencel, 60% bamboo viscose, 230 yd. / 210 m per 1.8 oz. / 50 g ball)

**OUTFIT DETAILS**
17473 Curry

Fingering weight (#1 super fine) yarn, shown in Hobbii *Friends Cotton 8/4* (100% cotton, 174 yd. / 160 m per 1.75 oz. / 50 g ball)

**SHAWL**
89 Deep Ocean

## FINISHED MEASUREMENTS

**HEIGHT:** 5.9 in. / 15 cm
**WIDTH:** 4.7 in. / 12 cm

## HOOK

- US B-1 / 2.0 mm crochet hook for the Body
- US C-2 / 2.5 mm crochet hook for the Hair

*Note: Everything is worked with US B-1 / 2.0 mm crochet hook except for the Hair, Beard, and Mustache.*

## NOTIONS

- Pair of 12 mm safety eyes
- Polyester stuffing
- Tapestry needle
- Removable stitch markers
- Sewing pins
- Pointy tweezers
- Craft glue
- Craft wire
- 4 small magnets (optional to stick the rock in Moses's hands)

## GAUGE

*Gauge is not critical for this project. Ensure your stitches are tight so the stuffing won't show through.*

For more information on how to make Moses, including tips, step-by-step pictures, and videos, scan this QR code!

## HEAD

With **Shell**.

**Rnd 1:** 6 sc in magic ring
**Rnd 2:** 6 inc [12]
**Rnd 3:** (1 sc, 1 inc) × 6 [18]
**Rnd 4:** 1 sc, 1 inc, (2 sc, 1 inc) × 5, 1 sc [24]
**Rnd 5:** (3 sc, 1 inc) × 6 [30]
**Rnd 6:** 2 sc, 1 inc, (4 sc, 1 inc) × 5, 2 sc [36]
**Rnd 7:** (5 sc, 1 inc) × 6 [42]
**Rnd 8:** 3 sc, 1 inc, (6 sc, 1 inc) × 5, 3 sc [48]
**Rnd 9:** 48 sc
**Rnd 10:** (5 sc, 1 inc) × 8 [56]
**Rnds 11–22:** 56 sc (12 rounds)
Insert the eyes between rounds 17 and 18, with 9 sc visible apart from each other.
**Rnd 23:** (5 sc, 1 dec) × 8 [48]
**Rnd 24:** 2 sc, 1 dec, (4 sc, 1 dec) × 7, 2 sc [40]
**Rnd 25:** 1 sc, 1 dec, (2 sc, 1 dec) × 9, 1 sc [30]
**Rnd 26:** (1 sc, 1 dec) × 10 [20]
Stuff the Head until round 26. You should not stuff from round 27 on.
**Rnd 27:** Blo 20 sc
**Rnds 28–35:** 20 sc (8 rounds)
**Rnd 36:** 10 dec [10]
Fasten off with an inverted magic ring.
Push the neck inward (from round 27 to 36) with the help of the hook handle.
For more instructions, see page 167.

## EARS (MAKE 2)

With **Shell**.

**Rnd 1:** 1 sc, 4 hdc, 1 sc in magic ring
Finish off and leave a long tail.

## NOSE

With **Shell**.
**Rnd 1:** 6 sc in magic ring
**Rnd 2:** (2 sc, 1 inc) × 2 [8]
Finish off and leave a long tail.

## EYEBROWS (MAKE 2)

With **Mercury**, make 6 chains and fasten off, leaving a long tail. Attach the Eyebrows with their outer corner 1 round above the eyes and the inner corner 2 rounds above the eyes, with a width of 4 sc.

To finish off, pass both ends through the Head having them leave in the same opening. Then, knot the ends together and push knot inside the Head to hide it.

## ROBE

With **Ruby**, make 36 chains and close them into a ring with 1 sc. This will be the first stitch of the round.
**Rnds 1–4:** 36 sc (4 rounds)
**Rnd 5:** (7 sc, 1 dec) × 4 [32]
**Rnds 6–8:** 32 sc (3 rounds)
**Rnd 9:** (14 sc, 1 dec) × 2 [30]
**Rnds 10–11:** 30 sc (2 rounds)
Don't fasten off, as we will continue crocheting it with the Body.

## LEFT LEG

With **Root Beer**.
We will work on both sides of the chains. Start with 5 chains and from the second chain from the hook make:

**Rnd 1:** 1 inc, 2 sc, in the last chain 4 sc, continue on the other side of the chains 2 sc, 1 inc [12]
**Rnd 2:** 2 inc, 2 sc, 4 inc, 2 sc, 2 inc [20]
**Rnd 3:** 20 BPsc
**Rnd 4:** 20 sc
**Rnd 5:** Change to **Shell**. Blo 20 sl st
**Rnd 6:** Insert the hook below both loops of the slip stitch. 20 sc
**Rnd 7:** 6 sc, 4 dec, 6 sc [16]
**Rnd 8:** 4 sc, 4 dec, 4 sc [12]
**Rnds 9–14:** 12 sc (6 rounds)
**Rnds 15–16:** Change to **Bridal White**. 12 sc (2 rounds)
Stuff the Leg and fasten off.
If you want your amigurumi to have flat feet to stand, make sure that you don't stuff it too much and leave it concave.

## RIGHT LEG

Repeat rounds 1 to 16 of the Left Leg.
Make **4 more sc** and **3 chains** to get to the side of the Leg.

## SANDALS

With **Root Beer**.
Attach the yarn to the 5th loop created by round 5. Make 22 chains, pass the chains around the ankle, skip 9 loops from the first st that you started, and attach the chains with 1 sl st. Fasten off.
Work Sandals on both feet before continuing with the Body.

## BODY

With **Bridal White**, we will continue the Body by joining both Legs. Be sure that both feet are facing forward at the junction of the Legs. Stuff the Body as you crochet.

**Rnd 17:** 12 sc, 3 sc on the chain, 12 sc, 3 sc on the chain [30]
**Rnds 18–22:** 30 sc (5 rounds)
Fasten off **Bridal White**. Place the Robe on the Body. Crochet both pieces together with **Ruby**.
**Rnd 23:** 30 sc (joining the Body and the Robe)
**Rnd 24:** (13 sc, 1 dec) × 2 [28]
**Rnd 25:** 28 sc
**Rnd 26:** 6 sc, 1 dec, 12 sc, 1 dec, 6 sc [26]
**Rnd 27:** (11 sc, 1 dec) × 2 [24]
**Rnds 28–29:** 24 sc (2 rounds)
**Rnd 30:** Flo 24 sl st
Fasten off.
Using the back loops of round 30, attach **Shell** and make:
**Rnd 31:** 24 sc
**Rnd 32:** 2 sc, 1 dec, (4 sc, 1 dec) × 3, 2 sc [20]
**Rnd 33:** (3 sc, 1 dec) × 4 [16]
**Rnds 34–40:** 16 sc (7 rounds)
**Rnd 41:** 8 dec [8]
Stuff the Body, fasten off, and leave a long tail to attach the Body and the Head.

## ARMS (MAKE 2)

With **Shell**.
**Rnd 1:** 6 sc in magic ring
**Rnd 2:** (2 sc, 1 inc) × 2 [8]
**Rnd 3:** 8 sc
**Rnd 4:** Change to **Ruby**. Blo 8 sl st
**Rnd 5:** Blo 8 sc
**Rnds 6–13:** 8 sc (8 rounds)
Put a magnet inside the Arms. Slightly stuff half of the Arms (until round 6). Pinch the Arm opening closed and crochet together with 4 sc. Leave a long tail to sew.

## HAIR

With **Mercury** and US C-2 / 2.5 mm hook.

**Rnd 1:** 6 sc in magic ring
**Rnd 2:** 6 inc [12]
**Rnd 3:** (1 sc, 1 inc) × 6 [18]
**Rnd 4:** 1 sc, 1 inc, (2 sc, 1 inc) × 5, 1 sc [24]
**Rnd 5:** (3 sc, 1 inc) × 6 [30]
**Rnd 6:** 2 sc, 1 inc, (4 sc, 1 inc) × 5, 2 sc [36]
**Rnd 7:** (5 sc, 1 inc) × 6 [42]
**Rnd 8:** 3 sc, 1 inc, (6 sc, 1 inc) × 5, 3 sc [48]

We will now crochet the strands of Hair around the 48 sc from round 8.

Make 27 chains, and from the third chain from the hook, make 25 hdc. Close the strand of Hair with 1 sl st in the following st. Sl st in the following stitch and repeat the sequence.

You should have 24 strands of Hair in total.

## BEARD

With **Mercury** and US C-2 / 2.5 mm hook, make 30 chains, and from the second chain from the hook:

**Row 1:** 29 sl st, chain and turn
**Row 2:** 5 sl st, 1 incT dc, 1 inc dc, 5 dc, 5 dtr, 5 dc, 1 inc dc, 1 incT dc, 5 sl st, chain and turn [35]
**Row 3:** 8 sl st, 7 hdc, 1 inc dc, 3 dc, 1 inc dc, 7 hdc, 8 sl st [37]

Leave a long tail.

## MUSTACHE

With **Mercury** and US C-2 / 2.5 mm hook, make 19 chains, and from the second chain from the hook:

**Row 1:** 18 sl st, chain and turn

**Row 2:** 1 sl st, 1 sc, 2 hdc, 2 dc, 2 tr, 2 sl st, 1 chain, 2 tr, 2 dc, 2 hdc, 1 sc, 1 sl st [18]

Leave a long tail.

## TABLET (MAKE 4)

With **Charcoal**, make 6 chains and from the second chain from the hook:

**Rnd 1:** 1 inc, 3 sc, 4 sc in the last chain, 3 sc, 1 inc [12]

**Rnd 2:** 1 sc, inc4sc, 3 sc, 4 inc, 3 sc, in4sc, 1 sc [24]

**Rnd 3:** 2 sc, inc3sc, 5 sc, (1 sc, 1 inc) × 4, 5 sc, inc3sc, 2 sc [32]

Leave a long tail for sewing on 2 pieces and fasten off the other 2. Place 2 pieces back-to-back and sew them together. Do not stuff it. Before closing, place a magnet inside the Tablet. This will make the Tablets stick to Moses's hands. You can also glue the Tablet to his hands if you prefer.

## SHAWL

With **Deep Ocean**.

Start with 57 chains, and from the second chain from the hook make:

**Row 1:** 56 sc, chain and turn

**Row 2:** Blo 26 sc, 2 dec, 26 sc, chain and turn [54]

**Rows 3–5:** Blo 54 sc, chain and turn (3 rows)

Fasten off.

## STAFF

Cut the craft wire to measure around 4 in. / 10 cm.

With **Black Coffee**, place a drop of glue at the tip of the Staff to fix the end, and wrap the yarn around the wire to cover it. Glue the opposite end to the Staff and cut the yarn.

## ASSEMBLY

Using a tapestry needle to attach the Head to the Body, pass the remaining yarn from the Head and the remaining yarn from the Body to the middle of the magic ring that started the Head.

Pull the two ends in order to adjust the Head to the Body, tie a knot and cut the tails. This way, the Head will be articulated.

Sew the Nose between rounds 17 and 18, between the eyes, leaving 3 sc distance from the Nose to the eyes.

Make the details on the Robe with **Curry**. Insert the crochet hook between rounds 1 and 2 of the Robe and crochet sl st between the rounds, making the stripes between rounds 1 and 2 and rounds 2 and 3. Fasten off.

Do the same on the Arms between rounds 5 and 6.

Sew the Arms between rounds 25 and 26, on the side of the Body, with 9 sc distant in the front part of the Body.

Insert the wire through both Arms: start at one hand, pass it through the Arm, then across the Body, and out through the opposite Arm until it reaches the other hand. This will allow Moses's Arms to stay open.

Place the Shawl over the shoulders of the amigurumi.

Place the Beard in a way that the sideburns start from round 15 to 18, and the flat bottom part is 3 rounds below the eyes.

Glue the Mustache just below the Nose.

Sew the Ears between rounds 16 and 18 (same line as the eyes), 3 sc apart from the eyes.

Make the details on the outer corner of the eyes with **Snow White**, see page 164.

If you want the eyes to be indented, see page 164.

**Note:** I always advise pinning every strand of Hair before applying glue. Just a drop of glue in each strand of Hair should be enough to fix it.

Place the Hair on the Head of your amigurumi, with the opposite side of the magic ring up.

Pin 16 strands of Hair around the Head, behind the Ears.

Make sure the remaining strands are evenly divided, 4 on each side, and gently swept backward.

After pinning all strands of Hair in the desired position, apply glue to each strand.

# The Story of David and Goliath

**1 Samuel 17: 1–57**

**As the Philistine army gathered for war against Israel, their champion, a giant named Goliath, stepped forward to mock King Saul's troops and challenge them to single combat. While the seasoned Israelite soldiers trembled in fear, David, a shepherd boy who had arrived at the camp to bring supplies, was moved by faith to accept Goliath's challenge. Rejecting the King's heavy armor, David approached the giant with only his staff, five smooth stones, and a sling, declaring that he fought in the name of the Lord:**

> Then said David to the Philistine, Thou comest to me with a sword, and with a spear, and with a shield: but I come to thee in the name of the Lord of hosts, the God of the armies of Israel, whom thou hast defied.[45] This day will the Lord deliver thee into mine hand; and I will smite thee, and take thine head from thee; and I will give the carcases of the host of the Philistines this day unto the fowls of the air, and to the wild beasts of the earth; that all the earth may know that there is a God in Israel.[46] And all this assembly shall know that the Lord saveth not with sword and spear: for the battle is the Lord's, and he will give you into our hands.[47] And it came to pass, when the Philistine arose, and came, and drew nigh to meet David, that David hastened, and ran toward the army to meet the Philistine.[48] And David put his hand in his bag, and took thence a stone, and slang it, and smote the Philistine in his forehead, that the stone sunk into his forehead; and he fell upon his face to the earth.[49] So David prevailed over the Philistine with a sling and with a stone, and smote the Philistine, and slew him; but there was no sword in the hand of David.[50]

**—1 Samuel 17:45–50**

The amigurumis of David and Goliath display an inspiring story, teaching us that courage, faith, and ingenuity can overcome overwhelming odds.

# David

## YARN

Fingering weight (#1 super fine) yarn, shown in Scheepjes *Catona* (100% mercerized cotton, 174 yd. / 125 m per 1.75 oz. / 50 g ball)

**SKIN**

255 Shell

**SHOES**

162 Black Coffee

**HAIR**

388 Rust

**EYE DETAIL**

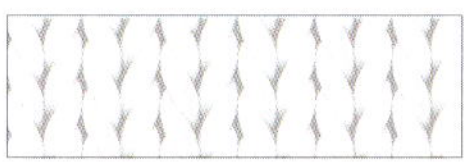

106 Snow White

**OUTFIT**

383 Ginger Gold

**STONE**

393 Charcoal

Fingering weight (#1 super fine) yarn, shown in Hobbii *Friends Cotton 8/4* (100% cotton, 174 yd. / 160 m per 1.75 oz. / 50 g ball)

**BELT/HEADBAND**

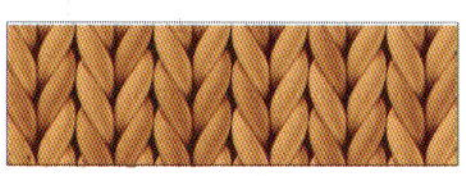

15 Walnut

## FINISHED MEASUREMENTS

**HEIGHT:** 5.3 in. / 13.5 cm
**WIDTH:** 2.75 in. / 7 cm

## HOOK

- US B-1 / 2.0 mm crochet hook for the Body
- US C-2 / 2.5 mm crochet hook for the Hair

*Note: Everything is worked with US B-1 / 2.0 mm crochet hook except for the Hair.*

## NOTIONS

- Pair of 11 mm safety eyes
- Polyester stuffing
- Tapestry needle
- Removable stitch markers
- Sewing pins
- Pointy tweezers
- Craft glue

## GAUGE

*Gauge is not critical for this project. Ensure your stitches are tight so the stuffing won't show through.*

For more information on how to make David, including tips, step-by-step pictures, and videos, scan this QR code!

## HEAD

With **Shell**.

**Rnd 1:** 6 sc in magic ring
**Rnd 2:** 6 inc [12]
**Rnd 3:** (1 sc, 1 inc) × 6 [18]
**Rnd 4:** 1 sc, 1 inc, (2 sc, 1 inc) × 5, 1 sc [24]
**Rnd 5:** (3 sc, 1 inc) × 6 [30]
**Rnd 6:** 2 sc, 1 inc, (4 sc, 1 inc) × 5, 2 sc [36]
**Rnd 7:** (5 sc, 1 inc) × 6 [42]
**Rnd 8:** 3 sc, 1 inc, (6 sc, 1 inc) × 5, 3 sc [48]
**Rnd 9:** (23 sc, 1 inc) × 2 [50]
**Rnds 10–20:** 50 sc (11 rounds)
Insert the eyes between rounds 15 and 16, with 9 sc visible apart from each other.
**Rnd 21:** (3 sc, 1 dec) × 10 [40]
**Rnd 22:** 1 sc, 1 dec, (2 sc, 1 dec) × 9, 1 sc [30]
**Rnd 23:** (1 sc, 1 dec) × 10 [20]
Stuff the Head until round 23. You should not stuff from round 24 on.
**Rnd 24:** Blo 20 sc
**Rnds 25–32:** 20 sc (8 rounds)
**Rnd 33:** 10 dec [10]
Fasten off with the inverted magic ring.
Push the neck inward (from round 24 to 33) with the help of the hook handle.
For more instructions, see page 167.

## EARS (MAKE 2)

With **Shell**.

**Rnd 1:** 1 sc, 1 hdc, 2 dc, 1 hdc, 1 sc in magic ring
Finish off and leave a long tail.

## NOSE

With **Shell**.

Embroider the Nose between **rounds 16** and **17**, leaving **3 sc** away from the eyes. Pass the yarn horizontally **3 times** at a distance of **3 sc**. Then, pass the same yarn several times vertically and fasten off.

## EYEBROWS (MAKE 2)

With **Rust**, make the Eyebrows with their outer corner 1 round above the eyes and the inner corner 2 rounds above the eyes, with a width of 4 sc.

## ROBE

With **Ginger Gold**, make 28 chains and close them into a ring with 1 sc. This will be the first stitch of the round.

**Rnds 1–6:** 28 sc (6 rounds)

**Rnd 7:** (12 sc, 1 dec) × 2 [26]

Don't fasten off, as we will continue crocheting it with the Body.

## LEFT LEG

With **Black Coffee**.

We will work on both sides of the chains. Start with 4 chains and from the second chain from the hook make:

**Rnd 1:** 1 inc, 1 sc, in the last chain 4 sc, continue on the other side of the chains 1 sc, 1 inc [10]

**Rnd 2:** 2 inc, 1 sc, 4 inc, 1 sc, 2 inc [18]

**Rnd 3:** 18 BPsc

**Rnd 4:** 18 sc

**Rnd 5:** Change to **Shell**. Blo 18 sl st

**Rnd 6:** Insert the hook below both loops of the slip stitch. 18 sc.

**Rnd 7:** 5 sc, 4 dec, 5 sc [14]

**Rnd 8:** 3 sc, 4 dec, 3 sc [10]

**Rnds 9–13:** 10 sc (5 rounds)

**Rnd 14:** Change to **Snow White**. 10 sc

Stuff the Leg and fasten off.

## RIGHT LEG

Repeat rounds 1 to 14 of the Left Leg.
Make **4 more sc** and **3 chains** to get to the side of the Leg.

## BODY

With **Snow White**, continue the Body by joining both Legs. Be sure that both feet are facing forward at the junction of the Legs. Stuff the Body as you crochet.
**Rnd 15:** 10 sc, 3 sc on the chain, 10 sc, 3 sc on the chain [26]
**Rnds 16–19:** 26 sc (4 rounds)
Fasten off **Snow White**. Place the Robe on the Body. Crochet both pieces together with **Ginger Gold**.
**Rnd 20:** 26 sc (joining the Body and the Robe)
**Rnds 21–24:** 26 sc (4 rounds)
**Rnd 25:** (11 sc, 1 dec) × 2 [24]
**Rnd 26:** 24 sc
**Rnd 27:** Flo 24 sc
Fasten off **Ginger Gold**.
Using the back loops of round 27, attach **Shell** and make:
**Rnd 27:** 24 sc
**Rnd 28:** 2 sc, 1 dec, (4 sc, 1 dec) × 3, 2 sc [20]
**Rnd 29:** (3 sc, 1 dec) × 4 [16]
**Rnds 30–35:** 16 sc (6 rounds)
**Rnd 36:** 8 dec [8]
Stuff the Body, fasten off, and leave a long tail to attach the Body and the Head.

## SANDALS (MAKE 2)

With **Black Coffee**.
Start on the fourth loop of round 4 from the Body. Attach the yarn and make 20 chains. Pass the chains around the Leg and close with a sl st on the 12th loop of the round. Fasten off.

## ARMS (MAKE 2)

With **Shell**.
**Rnd 1:** 7 sc in magic ring
**Rnds 2–3:** 7 sc (2 rounds)
**Rnd 4:** Change to **Ginger Gold**. 7 inc [14]
**Rnd 5:** 14 sc (2 rounds)
**Rnd 6:** 7 dec [7]
**Rnds 7–10:** 7 sc (4 rounds)
Slightly stuff half of the Arms (until round 5).
Pinch Arm opening closed and crochet together with 3 sc. Leave a long tail.

## HAIR

With **Rust**.
**Rnd 1:** 6 sc in magic ring
**Rnd 2:** Blo 6 inc [12]
**Rnd 3:** Blo (1 sc, 1 inc) × 6 [18]
**Rnd 4:** Blo 1 sc, 1 inc, (2 sc, 1 inc) × 5, 1 sc [24]
**Rnd 5:** Blo (3 sc, 1 inc) × 6 [30]
**Rnd 6:** Blo 2 sc, 1 inc, (4 sc, 1 inc) × 5, 2 sc [36]
**Rnd 7:** Blo (5 sc, 1 inc) × 6 [42]
**Rnd 8:** Blo 3 sc, 1 inc, (6 sc, 1 inc) × 5, 3 sc [48]
**Rnds 9–12:** Blo 48 sc (4 rounds)
**Rnds 13–14:** 48 sc (2 rounds)
**Rnd 15:** Blo 48 sc
Fasten off.

Attach the yarn on the first loop on top of the Head to make the curls. Make:
1sl, 3 chains and close with
1 sl st in the same loop.
1 sl st in the following loop.
Make this sequence in all the loops of the Hair, including round 15.
Fasten off.

## HEADBAND

With **Walnut**. Make 60 chains, and from the second chain from the hook 59 hdc.
Fasten off.

## BELT

With **Walnut**.
Make 52 chains and fasten off.

## SLING AND STONE

### Stone

With **Charcoal**.
**Rnd 1:** 6 sc in magic ring
**Rnd 2:** 6 inc [12]
**Rnds 3–4:** 12 sc (2 rounds)
**Rnd 5:** 6 dec [6]
Stuff the Stone with the help of the tweezers and close with an inverted magic ring. Fasten off.

### Sling

With **Black Coffee**. Make 22 chains and close them with 1 sc. This is the first st of the round.
**Rnd 1:** 8 sc, 6 dc, 8 sc [22]
Leave a tail to attach it to the Arms.

### ASSEMBLY

Using a tapestry needle attach the Head to the Body, pass the remaining tail of the Head and the remaining tail of the Body to the middle of the magic ring that started the Head.

Pull the two ends in order to adjust the Head to the Body, tie a knot and cut the tails. This way, the Head will be articulated.

Sew the Arms between rounds 25 and 26, on the side of the Body, with 9 sc distant in the front part of the Body.

Add the Belt.

Sew the Ears between rounds 14 and 16 (same line as the eyes), 4 sc apart from the eyes.

Make the details on the outer corner of the eyes with **Snow White**, see page 164.

If you want the eyes to be indented, see page 164.

**Note:** I always advise pinning every strand of Hair before applying glue. Just a drop of glue in each strand of Hair should be enough to fix it.

Place the Hair on the Head of your amigurumi.

Add the Headband in the gap created in the Hair, between rounds 13 and 14, and tie a knot.

Tie the remaining tails of the Sling to David's hands and put the Stone inside.

# Goliath

## YARN

Fingering weight (#1 super fine) yarn, shown in Scheepjes *Catona* (100% mercerized cotton, 174 yd. / 125 m per 1.75 oz. / 50 g ball)

**SKIN**

506 Caramel

**SHOES**

162 Black Coffee

**HAIR/BEARD**

110 Jet Black

**EYE DETAIL**

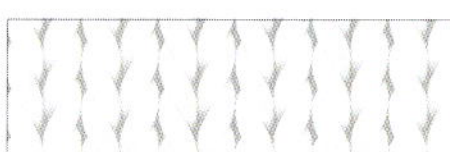

106 Snow White

**OUTFIT**

387 Dark Olive

**ARMOR/HELMET**

393 Charcoal

## FINISHED MEASUREMENTS

**HEIGHT:** 7.5 in. / 19 cm
**WIDTH:** 3.9 in. / 10 cm

## HOOK

- US B-1 / 2.0 mm crochet hook

## NOTIONS

- Pair of 13 mm safety eyes
- Polyester stuffing
- Tapestry needle
- Removable stitch markers
- Sewing pins
- Pointy tweezers
- Craft glue

## GAUGE

*Gauge is not critical for this project. Ensure your stitches are tight so the stuffing won't show through.*

For more information on how to make Goliath, including tips, step-by-step pictures, and videos, scan this QR code!

## HEAD

With **Caramel**.
**Rnd 1:** 6 sc in magic ring
**Rnd 2:** 6 inc [12]
**Rnd 3:** (1 sc, 1 inc) × 6 [18]
**Rnd 4:** 1 sc, 1 inc, (2 sc, 1 inc) × 5, 1 sc [24]
**Rnd 5:** (3 sc, 1 inc) × 6 [30]
**Rnd 6:** 2 sc, 1 inc, (4 sc, 1 inc) × 5, 2 sc [36]
**Rnd 7:** (5 sc, 1 inc) × 6 [42]
**Rnd 8:** 3 sc, 1 inc, (6 sc, 1 inc) × 5, 3 sc [48]
**Rnd 9:** (7 sc, 1 inc) × 6 [54]
**Rnd 10:** 4 sc, 1 inc, (8 sc, 1 inc) × 5, 4 sc [60]
**Rnds 11–23:** 60 sc (13 rounds)
Insert the eyes between rounds 18 and 19, with 9 sc visible apart from each other.
**Rnd 24:** 4 sc, 1 dec, (8 sc, 1 dec) × 5, 4 sc [54]
**Rnd 25:** (7 sc, 1 dec) × 6 [48]
**Rnd 26:** (5 sc, 1 dec) × 8 [40]
**Rnd 27:** 1 sc, 1 dec, (2 sc, 1 dec) × 9, 1 sc [30]
**Rnd 28:** (1 sc, 1 dec) × 10 [20]
Stuff the Head until round 28. Do not stuff from round 29 on.
**Rnd 29:** Blo 20 sc
**Rnds 30–36:** 20 sc (7 rounds)
**Rnd 37:** 10 dec [10]
Fasten off with an inverted magic ring.
Push the neck inward (from round 29 to 37) with the help of the hook handle.
For more instructions, see page 167.

## EARS (MAKE 2)

With **Caramel**, make a magic ring.
**Rnd 1:** In ring: 1 sc, 1 hdc, 2 dc, 1 hdc, 1 sc
Finish off and leave a long tail.

## NOSE

With **Caramel**.
**Rnd 1:** 8 sc in magic ring
**Rnd 2:** 8 sc
Leave a long tail.

## EYEBROWS (MAKE 2)

With **Jet Black**, make the Eyebrows with their outer corner 2 rounds above the eyes and the inner corner 1 round above the eyes, with a width of 4 sc.

## BEARD

With **Jet Black**.
Make 34 chains and from the second chain from the hook:
**Row 1:** 33 sl st, chain and turn
**Row 2:** 5 sl st, inc3 hdc, inc hdc, 19 dc, 1 inc hdc, inc3 hdc, 5 sl st [39]
1 chain and continue on the top part of the Beard
14 sl st, skip 6 st, 14 sl st
Leave a long tail.

## SKIRT

With **Dark Olive**. Make 10 chains and from the second chain from the hook make:
**Row 1:** 9 sc, chain and turn
**Rnds 2–36:** Blo 9 sc, chain and turn
Join both ends to close. Make 9 sc to close and form the Skirt.
Continue crocheting on the top part of the Skirt, as we will later join this to the Body.
Make 36 sc and do not fasten it off.

## LEFT LEG

With **Black Coffee**.
Work on both sides of the chains. Start with 4 chains and from the second chain from the hook make:
**Rnd 1:** 1 inc, 1 sc, in the last chain 4 sc, continue on the other side of the chains 1 sc, 1 inc [10]
**Rnd 2:** 2 inc, 1 sc, 4 inc, 1 sc, 2 inc [18]
**Rnd 3:** (1 sc, 1 inc) × 2, 1 sc, (1 sc, 1 inc) × 4, 1 sc, (1 sc, 1 inc) × 2 [26]
**Rnd 4:** 26 Bpsc
**Rnd 5:** 26 sc
**Rnd 6:** 9 sc, 4 dec, 9 sc [22]
**Rnd 7:** 7 sc, 4 dec, 7 sc [18]
**Rnd 8:** (7 sc, 1 dec) × 2 [16]
**Rnd 9:** 16 sc
**Rnd 10:** Flo 16 sl st
**Rnd 11:** Working on the back loops. Change to **Caramel**. 16 sc
**Rnds 12–17:** 16 sc (6 rounds)
**Rnd 18:** Change to **Snow White**. 16 sc
**Rnds 19–20:** 16 sc (2 rounds)
Stuff the Leg and fasten off.
If you want your amigurumi to have flat feet to stand, make sure that you don't stuff it too much and leave it concave.

## RIGHT LEG

Repeat rounds 1 to 17 of the Left Leg.

Make **4 more sc** and **2 chains** to get to the side of the Leg.

## BODY

With **Snow White**, continue the Body by joining both Legs. Be sure that both feet are facing forward at the junction of the Legs. Stuff the Body as you crochet.

**Rnd 20:** 16 sc, 2 sc on the chain, 16 sc, 2 sc on the chain [36]

**Rnds 21–27:** 36 sc (7 rounds)

Fasten off **Snow White**. Place Skirt on Body. Crochet both pieces together with **Dark Olive**. Continue stuffing as you crochet.

**Rnd 28:** 36 sc (joining the Body and the Skirt)

**Rnds 29–32:** 36 sc (4 rounds)

**Rnd 33:** (7 sc, 1 dec) × 4 [32]

**Rnds 34–38:** 32 sc (5 rounds)

**Rnd 39:** 1 sc, 1 dec, (2 sc, 1 dec) × 7, 1 sc [24]

**Rnd 40:** 24 sc

**Rnd 41:** Flo 24 sl st

Fasten off **Dark Olive**. Attach **Caramel** in the first back loop of round 41.

**Rnd 42:** 24 sc

**Rnd 43:** 2 sc, 1 dec, (4 sc, 1 dec) × 3, 2 sc [20]

**Rnd 44:** (3 sc, 1 dec) × 4 [16]

**Rnds 45–50:** 16 sc (6 rounds)

**Rnd 51:** 8 dec [8]

Stuff the Body, fasten off, and leave a long tail to attach the Body and the Head.

## ARMS (MAKE 2)

With **Caramel**.
**Rnd 1:** 6 sc in magic ring
**Rnd 2:** (1 sc, 1 inc) × 3 [9]
**Rnd 3:** 9 sc
**Rnd 4:** Inc3 hdc, 8 sc [11]
**Rnd 5:** Dec3 hdc, 8 sc [9]
**Rnds 6–8:** 9 sc (3 rounds)
**Rnd 9:** (2 sc, 1 inc) × 3 [12]
**Rnds 10–11:** 12 sc (2 rounds)
**Rnd 12:** (2 sc, 1 inc) × 4 [16]
Slightly stuff half of the Arms (until round 6) and fasten off.

## SLEEVES (MAKE 2)

With **Dark Olive**. Make 16 chains and close them with 1 sc. This will be the first st of the round.
**Rnds 1–2:** 16 sc (2 rounds)
Put the Arms inside the Sleeves. We will now crochet both pieces together.
**Rnd 3:** 16 sc (joining both pieces)
**Rnd 4:** 16 sc
**Rnd 5:** 8 dec [8]
Make the inverted magic ring and fasten off, leaving a long tail to sew.

## HAIR

With **Jet Black**.
**Rnd 1:** 6 sc in magic ring
**Rnd 2:** 6 inc [12]
**Rnd 3:** (1 sc, 1 inc) × 6 [18]
**Rnd 4:** 1 sc, 1 inc, (2 sc, 1 inc) × 5, 1 sc [24]
**Rnd 5:** (3 sc, 1 inc) × 6 [30]
**Rnd 6:** 2 sc, 1 inc, (4 sc, 1 inc) × 5, 2 sc [36]
**Rnd 7:** (5 sc, 1 inc) × 6 [42]
**Rnd 8:** 3 sc, 1 inc, (6 sc, 1 inc) × 5, 3 sc [48]
**Rnd 9:** (7 sc, 1 inc) × 6 [54]
**Rnd 10:** 4 sc, 1 inc, (8 sc, 1 inc) × 5, 4 sc [60]
**Rnd 11:** 60 sc
From now on, we will work in rows, always turning the piece to continue crocheting.
**Note:** I prefer to turn without making the chain here to have a better finish, but you can also chain and turn, if you prefer it that way.
**Row 12:** 29 sc, 1 sl st, turn [30]
**Row 13:** 1 sl st, 58 sc, 1 sc, turn [60]
**Row 14:** 1 sl st, 49 sc, turn [50]
**Row 15:** 40 sc, turn
**Row 16:** Skip the first st, 37 sc, skip 1 st, 1 sc, turn [38]
**Row 17:** 38 sc, turn
**Row 18:** Skip the first st, 35 sc, skip 1 st, 1 sc, turn [36]
**Rows 19–26:** 36 sc, turn (8 rows)
Fasten off.

## SPEAR

Start with **Black Coffee**.
**Rnd 1:** 6 sc in magic ring
**Rnds 2–33:** 6 sc (32 rounds)
**Rnd 34:** Change to **Charcoal**. FPsc 6 inc [12]
**Rnd 35:** (1 sc, 1 inc) × 6 [18]
Insert a piece of craft wire to make it firm. Do not stuff the cable part of the Spear.
**Rnd 36:** 18 BPsc
**Rnds 37–38:** 18 sc (2 rounds)
**Rnd 39:** Dec, 5 sc, 2 dec, 5 sc, dec [14]
**Rnds 40–41:** 14 sc (2 rounds)
**Rnd 42:** Dec, 3 sc, 2 dec, 3 sc, dec [10]
**Rnds 43–44:** 10 sc (2 rounds)
**Rnd 45:** Dec, 1 sc, 2 dec, 1 sc, dec [6]
**Rnd 46:** 6 sc
Stuff the triangle part of the Spear and fasten off.

## ARMOR (PART I)

With **Charcoal**.

Start with 8 chains, and from the second chain from the hook, make:

**Row 1:** 7 sc, turn

**Rows 2–7:** 7 sc, turn (6 rounds)

Now we will crochet around this square piece.

Make (1 chain, 7 sc) × 3

Make 12 chains, and from the second chain from the hook, make 11 hdc. 6 sl st on the square.

Make 12 chains, and from the second chain from the hook, 11 hdc. Close it with 1 sl st and fasten off.

## ARMOR (PART II)

**Row 1:** 7 sc, turn
**Rows 2–7:** 7 sc, turn (6 rounds)
Now we will crochet around this square piece.
Make (1 chain, 7 sc) × 4.
Make 30 chains and attach the chains in the opposite side of the square with a sl st, to form a ring. This will be the first st from now on, as this ring will be the belt of the armour.
**Rnds 1–3:** 37 sc (3 rounds)
Fasten off.

### HELMET (PART I)

With **Charcoal**.
**Rnd 1:** 6 sc in magic ring
**Rnd 2:** 6 inc [12]
**Rnd 3:** (1 sc, 1 inc) × 6 [18]
**Rnd 4:** 1 sc, 1 inc, (2 sc, 1 inc) × 5, 1 sc [24]
**Rnd 5:** (3 sc, 1 inc) × 6 [30]
**Rnd 6:** 2 sc, 1 inc, (4 sc, 1 inc) × 5, 2 sc [36]
**Rnd 7:** (5 sc, 1 inc) × 6 [42]
**Rnd 8:** 3 sc, 1 inc, (6 sc, 1 inc) × 5, 3 sc [48]
**Rnd 9:** (7 sc, 1 inc) × 6 [54]
**Rnd 10:** 4 sc, 1 inc, (8 sc, 1 inc) × 5, 4 sc [60]
**Rnd 11:** (14 sc, 1 inc) × 4 [64]
**Rnds 12–17:** 64 sc (6 rounds)
**Rnd 18:** Flo 64 sc
**Rnd 19:** 64 sc
Fasten off.

### HELMET (PART II)

With **Charcoal**.
Make 2 cords with 25 chains each and leave a long tail.
These cords go from one side of the helmet to the other. Pin them in place before sewing.

### HELMET (PART III)

With **Charcoal**.
**Rnd 1:** 6 sc in magic ring
**Rnd 2:** 6 inc [12]
Leave a long tail.
Place Part III on top of the cords (Part II), at the crown of the Helmet. Sew it securely. Secure the cords to the Helmet, ensuring they form a **cross on top of the Head**.

## ASSEMBLY

Sew the Nose between rounds 18 and 20, between the eyes.

Sew the Ears between rounds 17 and 19, 4 stitches away from the eyes.

If you want the eyes to be indented, see page 164.

Make the details on the outer corner of the eyes with **Snow White**, see page 164.

Place the sideburns from round 15 on, and the Beard below the eyes. Once you have it in the right position, sew the top part of the Beard and the sideburns to the Head.

Place the Armor Part II with the square part on the front part of the Body.

Place Part I of the Armor on the back and pass the Straps to the front of the Armor. Either sew or glue this part together.

Sew the Arms below the Straps of the Armor, on the sides of the Body. Make sure that the thumbs of the amigurumi are facing up when sewing.

Using a tapestry needle to attach the Head to the Body, pass the remaining tail of the Head and the remaining tail of the Body to the middle of the magic ring that started the Head.

Pull the two ends in order to adjust the Head to the Body, tie a knot and cut the tails. This way, the Head will be articulated.

Place the Hair on the Head and glue it.

"And all this assembly shall know that the Lord saveth not with sword and spear: for the battle is the Lord's, and he will give you into our hands."

—1 Samuel 17:47

# The Story of Samson and Delilah

Judges 14–16

**Gifted with supernatural strength so long as he kept his Nazirite vow never to cut his hair, Samson became a legendary judge of Israel who single-handedly thwarted the Philistine armies. However, his downfall began when he fell in love with a woman named Delilah, who was bribed by Philistine leaders to uncover the secret of his might. After multiple failed attempts to deceive her, Samson finally reveals that his strength lay in his hair. Here we see our Delilah lulling him to sleep, after which she ordered a servant to cut his hair. Stripped of his power, Samson was blinded by his enemies and abandoned by the Lord. Eventually, though, his hair began to grow back. Our Samson, chains around his wrists, is shown in his final act:**

> And Samson called unto the Lord, and said, O Lord God, remember me, I pray thee, and strengthen me, I pray thee, only this once, O God, that I may be at once avenged of the Philistines for my two eyes.[28] And Samson took hold of the two middle pillars upon which the house stood, and on which it was borne up, of the one with his right hand, and of the other with his left.[29] And Samson said, Let me die with the Philistines. And he bowed himself with all his might; and the house fell upon the lords, and upon all the people that were therein. So the dead whichhe slew at his death were more than they which he slew in his life.[30]

**—Judges 16:28–30**

Samson's story is one of the dangers of misplaced trust, and breaking vows. How the mighty can fall!

# Samson

## YARN

Fingering weight (#1 super fine) yarn, shown in Scheepjes *Catona* (100% mercerized cotton, 174 yd. / 125 m per 1.75 oz. / 50 g ball)

**SKIN**
502 Camel

**HAIR**
110 Jet Black

**SHOES/VEST**
507 Chocolate

**EYE DETAIL**
106 Snow White

**OUTFIT**
525 Fir

**HEADBAND/DETAILS**
388 Rust

Any standard black embroidery thread can be used for the eyebrows.

## FINISHED MEASUREMENTS

**HEIGHT:** 5.9 in. / 15 cm
**WIDTH:** 3.15 in. / 8 cm

## HOOK

- US B-1 / 2.0 mm crochet hook for the Body
- US C-2 / 2.5 mm crochet hook for the Hair

*Note: Everything is worked with US B-1 / 2.0 mm crochet hook except for the Hair.*

## NOTIONS

- Pair of 13 mm safety eyes
- Polyester stuffing
- Tapestry needle
- Removable stitch markers
- Sewing pins
- Pointy tweezers
- Craft glue

## GAUGE

*Gauge is not critical for this project. Ensure your stitches are tight so the stuffing won't show through.*

For more information on how to make Samson, including tips, step-by-step pictures, and videos, scan this QR code!

## RIGHT LEG

Repeat rounds 1 to 19 of the Left Leg.
Make **3 more sc** and **2 chains** to get to the side of the Leg.

## BODY

We will continue the Body by joining both Legs. Be sure that both feet are facing forward at the junction of the Legs. Stuff the Body as you crochet.

**Rnd 20:** 16 sc, 2 sc on the chain, 16 sc, 2 sc on the chain [36]
**Rnds 21–24:** 36 sc (4 rounds)
**Rnd 25:** (7 sc, 1 dec) × 4 [32]
**Rnd 26:** Change to **Fir**. 32 sc
**Rnd 27:** 32 sc
**Rnd 28:** Change to **Camel**. Blo 32 sc
**Rnd 29:** Blo 7 sc, 2 inc, 14 sc, 2 inc, 7 sc [36]
**Rnd 30:** 36 sc
**Rnd 31:** 8 sc, 2 inc, 16 sc, 2 inc, 8 sc [40]
**Rnds 32–36:** 40 sc (5 rounds)
Continue stuffing the Body. We will now join the Arms, making sure the biceps are facing up.
**Rnd 37:** 7 sc, 4 sc joining the Arm to the Body, 16 sc, 4 sc joining the Arm to the Body, 9 sc [40]
**Note:** Depending on your stitch direction and tension, your stitches may naturally lean to one side. To keep the Arms placed symmetrically, you may need to adjust the number of stitches at the beginning and end of this round. Shift a few stitches if needed so both Arms are aligned evenly on the Body.

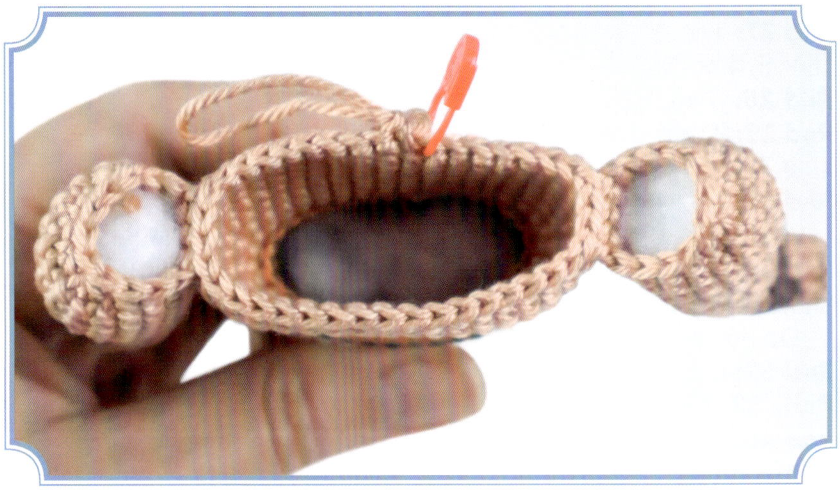

**Rnd 38:** 7 sc, 12 sc around the Arm, 16 sc, 12 sc around the Arm, 9 sc [56]
**Rnd 39:** (5 sc, 1 dec) × 8 [48]
**Rnd 40:** 2 sc, 1 dec, (4 sc, 1 dec) × 7, 2 sc [40]
**Rnd 41:** 40 sc
**Rnd 42:** (3 sc, 1 dec) × 8 [32]
**Rnd 43:** 1 sc, 1 dec, (2 sc, 1 dec) × 7, 1 sc [24]
**Rnds 44–45:** 24 sc (2 rounds)
**Rnd 46:** (2 sc, 1 dec) × 6 [18]
**Rnd 47:** (7 sc, 1 dec) × 2 [16]
**Rnds 48–53:** 16 sc (6 rounds)
**Rnd 54:** 8 dec [8]
Make sure that the neck (from rounds 48 to 54) is firm.

## SHOES

With **Chocolate**.

Insert the crochet hook in the 8th loop of round 6. Make 28 chains, pass the chains around the ankle, and attach with 1 sl st in the 18th loop. Make 8 chains and attach them with 1 sl st back in the 8th stitch again.

## SKIRT

Turn the Body upside down and, with **Fir**, attach it to the last frontal loop of round 27 of the Body. Make:

**Rnd 1:** 32 sc
**Rnd 2:** (7 sc, 1 inc) × 4 [36]
**Rnd 3:** 4 sc, 1 inc, (8 sc, 1 inc) × 3, 4 sc [40]
**Rnd 4:** (9 sc, 1 inc) × 4 [44]
**Rnds 5–10:** 44 sc (6 rounds)
**Rnd 11:** 44 sl st
Fasten off.

## HAIR

With **Jet Black** and US C-2 / 2.5 mm hook.

We will crochet an oval piece from the foundation chain, by working on both sides of the chains.

Make 12 chains, and from the second chain from the hook, make:

1 inc, 9 sc, 4 sc in the last one, 9 sc, 1 inc [26]

Work around the 26 st, and make 1 strand of Hair in each of them. Make:

40 chains, and from the second chain from the hook make:

(2 hdc, 1 inc hdc) × 8, 15 hdc.

Close the strand of Hair with 1 sl st in the following st and restart the sequence.

You should have 26 strands of Hair.

## VEST

With **Chocolate**. Make 31 chains and from the second chain from the hook, make:

**Row 1:** 30 sc, turn

**Row 2:** 3 sc, inc3, 5 sc, inc3, 10 sc, inc3, 5 sc, inc3, 3 sc, turn [38]

**Row 3:** 4 sc, inc3, 7 sc, inc3, 12 sc, inc3, 7 sc, inc3, 4 sc, turn [46]

**Row 4:** 5 sc, 8 chains, skip 11 sc, 14 sc, 8 chains, skip 11 sc, 5 sc, turn [40]

**Row 5:** 40 sc, turn

**Row 6:** 1 inc, 39 sc, turn [41]

**Row 7:** 41 sc, turn

**Row 8:** 1 inc, 40 sc, turn [42]

**Row 9:** 42 sc, turn

**Row 10:** Inc, 41 sc, turn [43]

**Row 11:** 43 sc, turn

**Row 12:** Inc, 42 sc, turn [44]

**Rows 13–15:** 44 sc, turn (3 rows)

To finish the Vest, work a round of sc all the way around the piece and fasten off. Do the same around both armholes openings.

## BELT

With **Rust**. Make 90 chains, then starting from the second chain from the hook, crochet 89 sl st. Fasten off. Wrap Belt twice around the waist and knot.

**Note:** I strongly recommend measuring it around your doll's waist, as you may need more (or fewer) stitches depending on your crochet tension.

## HEADBAND

With **Rust**. Make 80 chains, then starting from the second chain from the hook, crochet 79 hdc.

Fasten off.

**Note:** I strongly recommend measuring it around your doll's Head, as you may need more (or fewer) stitches depending on your crochet tension.

## ASSEMBLY

Using a tapestry needle to attach the Head to the Body, pass the remaining tail of the Head and the remaining tail of the Body to the middle of the magic ring that started the Head.

Pull the two ends in order to adjust the Head to the Body, tie a knot and cut the tails. This way, the Head will be articulated.

Sew the Ears between rounds 18 and 21 (same line as the eyes), 3 sc apart from the eyes.

Make the details on the outer corner of the eyes with **Snow White**, see page 164.

If you want the eyes to be indented, see page 164.

With the **Black** embroidery thread, make the eyebrows with their outer corner 1 round above the eyes and the inner corner 2 rounds above the eyes, with a width of 4 sc.

Place the Vest on the figure and wrap the Belt on top of it. Tie a knot to secure the Belt on the Body.

**Note:** I always advise pinning every strand of Hair before applying glue. Just a drop of glue in each strand of Hair should be enough to fix it.

Place the Hair on the Head. The oval piece, which is the foundation of the Hair, should be on the top of the Head.

Split the Hair so you have 13 strands for each side. Leave 4 strands of Hair loose in front of the Ears (8 strands in total).

Pin the remaining strands of Hair around the Head, behind the Ears. You will have 18 strands of Hair.

Place the Headband on the Head and tie a knot at the back to fix it.

Make sure the remaining strands of Hair are evenly divided, 4 on each side, and gently swept backward. These remaining strands of Hair are placed on top of the Headband.

# Delilah

## YARN

Fingering weight (#1 super fine) yarn, shown in Scheepjes *Catona* (100% mercerized cotton, 174 yd. / 125 m per 1.75 oz. / 50 g ball)

**SKIN**

502 Camel

**HAIR**

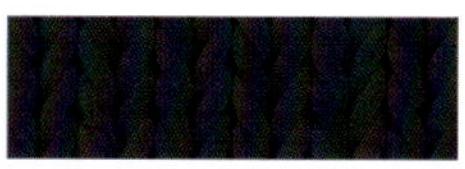

110 Jet Black

**EYE DETAIL**

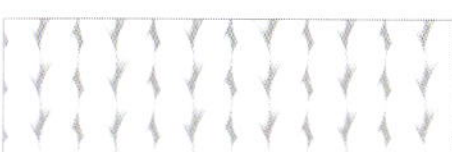

106 Snow White

**DRESS**

128 Tyrian Purple

Fingering weight (#1 super fine) yarn, shown in Hobbii *Friends Cotton 8/4* (100% cotton, 174 yd. / 160 m per 1.75 oz. / 50 g ball)

**SHOES**

13 Ochre

Any standard black embroidery thread can be used for eyebrows and eyelashes.

Fingering weight (#1 super fine) yarn, shown in Hobbii *Tencel Bamboo Fine* (40% Tencel, 60% bamboo viscose, 230 yd. / 210 m per 1.8 oz. / 50 g ball)

**CROWN/ DRESS DETAILS**

17473 Curry

## FINISHED MEASUREMENTS

**HEIGHT:** 5.9 in. / 15 cm
**WIDTH:** 3.15 in. / 8 cm

## HOOK

- US B-1 / 2.0 mm crochet hook for the Body
- US C-2 / 2.5 mm crochet hook for the Hair

***Note:*** *Everything is worked with US B-1 / 2.0 mm crochet hook except for the Hair.*

## NOTIONS

- Pair of 13 mm safety eyes
- Polyester stuffing
- Tapestry needle
- Removable stitch markers
- Sewing pins
- Pointy tweezers
- Craft glue

## GAUGE

*Gauge is not critical for this project. Ensure your stitches are tight so the stuffing won't show through.*

For more information on how to make Delilah, including tips, step-by-step pictures, and videos, scan this QR code!

## HEAD

With **Camel**.

**Rnd 1:** 6 sc in magic ring
**Rnd 2:** 6 inc [12]
**Rnd 3:** (1 sc, 1 inc) × 6 [18]
**Rnd 4:** 1 sc, 1 inc, (2 sc, 1 inc) × 5, 1 sc [24]
**Rnd 5:** (3 sc, 1 inc) × 6 [30]
**Rnd 6:** 2 sc, 1 inc, (4 sc, 1 inc) × 5, 2 sc [36]
**Rnd 7:** (5 sc, 1 inc) × 6 [42]
**Rnd 8:** 3 sc, 1 inc, (6 sc, 1 inc) × 5, 3 sc [48]
**Rnd 9:** 48 sc
**Rnd 10:** (5 sc, 1 inc) × 8 [56]
**Rnds 11–22:** 56 sc (12 rounds)
Insert the eyes between rounds 17 and 18, with 9 sc visible apart from each other.
**Rnd 23:** (5 sc, 1 dec) × 8 [48]
**Rnd 24:** 2 sc, 1 dec, (4 sc, 1 dec) × 7, 2 sc [40]
**Rnd 25:** 1 sc, 1 dec, (2 sc, 1 dec) × 9, 1 sc [30]
**Rnd 26:** (1 sc, 1 dec) × 10 [20]
Stuff the Head until round 26. Do not stuff from round 27 on.
**Rnd 27:** Blo 20 sc
**Rnds 28–35:** 20 sc (8 rounds)
**Rnd 36:** 10 dec [10]
Fasten off with the inverted magic ring.
Push the neck inward (from round 27 to 36) with the help of the hook handle.
For more instructions, see page 167.

## EARS (MAKE 2)

With **Shell**.

**Rnd 1:** 1 sc, 4 hdc, 1 sc in magic ring
Finish off and leave a long tail.

## NOSE

With **Camel**.

Embroider the Nose between **rounds 18** and **19**, leaving **3 sc** away from the eyes. Pass the yarn horizontally **4 times** at a distance of **3 sc**. Then, pass the same yarn several times vertically and fasten off.

## LEFT LEG

With **Ochre**.

Work on both sides of the chains. Start with 5 chains and from the second chain from the hook make:
**Rnd 1:** 1 inc, 2 sc, in the last chain 4 sc, continue on the other side of the chains 2 sc, 1 inc [12]
**Rnd 2:** 2 inc, 2 sc, 4 inc, 2 sc, 2 inc [20]
**Rnd 3:** 20 BPsc
**Rnd 4:** 20 sc
**Rnd 5:** Change to **Camel**. Blo 20 sl st
**Rnd 6:** Insert the hook below both loops of the slip stitch. 20 sc
**Rnd 7:** 6 sc, 4 dec, 6 sc [16]
**Rnd 8:** 4 sc, 4 dec, 4 sc [12]
**Rnds 9–14:** 12 sc (6 rounds)
**Rnd 15:** Change to **Snow White**. 12 sc
Stuff the Leg and fasten off.
If you want your amigurumi to have flat feet to stand, make sure that you don't stuff it too much and leave it concave.

## RIGHT LEG

Repeat rounds 1 to 15 of the Left Leg.
Make **3 more sc** and **3 chains** to get to the side of the Leg.

## BODY

We will continue the Body by joining both Legs. Be sure that both feet are facing forward at the junction of the Legs. Stuff the Body as you crochet.
**Rnd 16:** 12 sc, 3 sc on the chain, 12 sc, 3 sc on the chain [30]
**Rnds 17–20:** 30 sc (4 rounds)
**Rnd 21:** Change to **Tyrian Purple**. 30 sc
**Rnd 22:** (13 sc, 1 dec) × 2 [28]
**Rnd 23:** 28 sc
**Rnd 24:** Blo 6 sc, 1 dec, 12 sc, 1 dec, 6 sc [26]
**Rnd 25:** 26 sc
**Rnd 26:** (11 sc, 1 dec) × 2 [24]
**Rnd 27:** 24 sc
**Rnd 28:** Change to **Camel**. 24 sc
**Rnd 29:** 24 sc
**Rnd 30:** 1 sc, 1 dec, (2 sc, 1 dec) × 5, 1 sc [18]
**Rnd 31:** 18 sc
**Rnd 32:** (7 sc, 1 dec) × 2 [16]
**Rnds 33–38:** 16 sc (6 rounds)
**Rnd 39:** 8 dec [8]
Stuff the Body, fasten off, and leave a long tail to attach the Body and the Head.

## SHOES

With **Ochre**.

Place the feet upside down. Attach the yarn to the last loop of round 5. Make:

**Rnd 1:** 7 sl st, 6 dc, 7 sl st [20] – Fasten off.

*The 6 dc should be on the front part of the Shoes. You can adjust the number of sl st before and after the dc, as long as you have 20 st at the end.

## ARMS (MAKE 2)

With **Camel**.

**Rnd 1:** 4 sc in magic ring

**Rnd 2:** 4 inc [8]

**Rnd 3:** 8 sc

**Rnd 4:** Change to **Tyrian Purple**. Blo 8 sl st

**Rnd 5:** Blo 8 sc

**Rnds 6–11:** 8 sc (6 rounds)

Slightly stuff half of the Arms (until round 5).

Pinch Arm opening closed and crochet together with 4 sc. Leave a long tail.

## DRESS

Turn the Body upside down and with **Tyrian Purple**, attach it to the last front loop of round 24 of the Body. Make:

**Rnd 1:** 3 sc, 1 inc, (6 sc, 1 inc) × 3, 3 sc [32]

**Rnd 2:** (7 sc, 1 inc) × 4 [36]

**Rnd 3:** (Flo 5 sc, Blo 1 sc) × 6 [36]

**Rnd 4:** [Flo (2 sc, 1 inc, 2 sc), Blo 1 sc] × 6 [42]

**Rnd 5:** (Flo 6 sc, Blo 1 sc) × 6 [42]

**Rnd 6:** [Flo (1 inc, 4 sc, 1 inc), Blo 1 sc] × 6 [54]

**Rnds 7–12:** (Flo 8 sc, Blo 1 sc) × 6 [54] (6 rounds)

Fasten off.

## HAIR

With **Jet Black** and US C-2 / 2.5 mm hook.

**Rnd 1:** 6 sc in magic ring

**Rnd 2:** 6 inc [12]

**Rnd 3:** (1 sc, 1 inc) × 6 [18]

**Rnd 4:** 1 sc, 1 inc, (2 sc, 1 inc) × 5, 1 sc [24]

Now we will crochet the strands of Hair.

**Strnds 1–4:** 22 chains, and from the third chain from the hook make 20 hdc. Close the strand of Hair with 1 sl st in the following st.

**Strnd 5:** 48 chains, and from the third chain from the hook make 46 hdc. Close the strand of Hair with 1 sl st in the following st.

**Strnd 6:** 48 chains, and from the third chain from the hook make 46 hdc. Close the strand of Hair with 1 sl st **in the same base stitch of strand 5**.

**Strnd 7:** 48 chains, and from the third chain from the hook make 46 hdc. Close the strand of Hair with 1 sl st in the following st.

**Strnd 8:** 48 chains, and from the third chain from the hook make 46 hdc. Close the strand of Hair with 1 sl st **in the same base stitch of strand 7**.

**Strnd 9:** 48 chains, and from the third chain from the hook make 46 hdc. Close the strand of Hair with 1 sl st in the following st.

**Strnd 10:** 48 chains, and from the third chain from the hook make 46 hdc. Close the strand of Hair with 1 sl st in the same base stitch of strand 9.

**Strnds 11–14:** 22 chains, and from the third chain from the hook make 20 hdc. Close the strand of Hair with 1 sl st in the following st.

**Strnds 15–16:** 12 chains, and from the third chain from the hook make 10 hdc. Close the strand of Hair with 1 sl st in the following st.

**Strnd 17:** 14 chains, and from the third chain from the hook make 12 hdc. Close the strand of Hair with 1 sl st in the following st.

**Strnd 18:** 16 chains, and from the third chain from the hook make 14 hdc. Close the strand of Hair with 1 sl st in the following st.

**Strnds 19–20:** 18 chains, and from the third chain from the hook make 16 hdc. Close the strand of Hair with 1 sl st in the following st.

**Strnd 21:** 16 chains, and from the third chain from the hook make 14 hdc. Close the strand of Hair with 1 sl st in the following st.

**Strnd 22:** 14 chains, and from the third chain from the hook make 12 hdc. Close the strand of Hair with 1 sl st in the following st.

**Strnds 23–24:** 12 chains, and from the third chain from the hook make 10 hdc. Close the strand of Hair with 1 sl st in the following st.

## CROWN

With **Curry**.

Make 22 chains and from the second chain from the hook make:

**Rnd 1:** 10 sc, 1 inc, 10 sc, chain and turn [22]

**Rnd 2:** 10 sc, 2 inc, 10 sc [24]

Leave a long tail.

## ASSEMBLY

Insert the crochet hook in the back of the amigurumi, between rounds 24 and 25.

Crochet 26 sl st around the waist with **Curry** and fasten off.

Sew the Arms between rounds 29 and 30, on the side of the Body, with 9 sc distant in the front part of the Body.

Make 38 chains with **Curry** and glue them on the entire upper part of the Dress: over the purple back and front part of the Dress and over the Arms, making a square shape in the front and back.

Pin every part of it before applying glue.

Using a tapestry needle to attach the Head to the Body, pass the remaining tail of the Head and the remaining tail of the Body to the middle of the magic ring that started the Head.

Pull the two ends in order to adjust the Head to the Body, tie a knot and cut the tails. This way, the Head will be articulated.

Sew the Ears between rounds 16 and 18 (same line as the eyes), 3 sc apart from the eyes.

Make the details on the outer corner of the eyes with **Snow White**. See page 164.

If you want the eyes to be indented, see instructions on page 164.

Using the **Black** embroidery thread, make the eyebrows with their outer corner 1 round above the eyes and the inner corner 2 rounds above the eyes, with a width of 4 sc.

Make the eyelashes on top of the eyes using the same embroidery thread.

**Note:** I always advise pinning every strand of Hair before applying glue. Just a drop of glue in each strand of Hair should be enough to fix it.

Put the Hair on the top of the Head with the opposite side of the magic ring up.

The long strands must be in the back, as they are going to be the braids.

Strands 15 and 24 should be on top of the Ears.

Strands 1 to 4 and 11 to 14 should be right behind he Ears.

Braid strands 5 to 10, using 2 strands together when braiding them. Sew or glue the end of the braids in order to secure them.

Leave strands 16 to 23 in the front of the face.

Place the Crown on top of the Head, between strands 15 and 16, and 23 and 24.

Adjust the remaining strands of Hair on the Head to make the bangs, 4 strands to the right and 4 strands to the left.

"There are six things that the Lord hates, seven that are an abomination to him: haughty eyes, a lying tongue, and hands that shed innocent blood, a heart that devises wicked plans, feet that make haste to run to evil, a false witness who breathes out lies, and one who sows discord among brothers."

—Proverbs 6:16–19

# Prophets and Faithful Servants

# The Story of Daniel in the Lion's Den

Daniel 6:1–28

**In the kingdom of Babylon, the prophet Daniel rose to high status under King Darius, making the other nobles in the city jealous. So, they tricked Darius into signing a decree that prohibited praying to anyone but the monarch. Despite the law, Daniel remained steadfast in his faith, praying to God openly three times a day. Daniel was arrested and sentenced to death, cast down into a pit of ravenous lions. Distraught, Darius watched as a stone was set on top of the pit, trapping Daniel with the lions inside. The amigurumis depict Daniel praying surrounded by the lions.**

> Then the king arose very early in the morning, and went in haste unto the den of lions.[19] And when he came to the den, he cried with a lamentable voice unto Daniel: and the king spake and said to Daniel, O Daniel, servant of the living God, is thy God, whom thou servest continually, able to deliver thee from the lions?[20] Then said Daniel unto the king, O king, live for ever.[21] My God hath sent his angel, and hath shut the lions' mouths, that they have not hurt me: forasmuch as before him innocency was found in me; and also before thee, O king, have I done no hurt.[22] Then was the king exceedingly glad for him, and commanded that they should take Daniel up out of the den. So Daniel was taken up out of the den, and no manner of hurt was found upon him, because he believed in his God.[23]
>
> **—Daniel 6:19–23**

Daniel's steadfast faith, especially in the face of such adversity, is a testament to the power of prayer.

# Daniel

## YARN

Fingering weight (#1 super fine) yarn, shown in Scheepjes *Catona* (100% mercerized cotton, 174 yd. / 125 m per 1.75 oz. / 50 g ball)

**SKIN**

157 Root Beer

**HAIR**

110 Jet Black

**EYE DETAIL**

106 Snow White

**OUTFIT**

124 Ultramarine

## FINISHED MEASUREMENTS

**HEIGHT:** 5.5 in. / 14 cm

**WIDTH:** 3.15 in. / 8 cm

## HOOK

- US B-1 / 2.0 mm crochet hook

## NOTIONS

- Pair of 13 mm safety eyes
- Polyester stuffing
- Tapestry needle
- Removable stitch markers
- Sewing pins
- Pointy tweezers
- Craft glue
- Craft wire

***Note:*** *We will add small stones to give weight to the feet so the amigurumi can balance and stay on its knees. You can use aquarium gravel or any other clean, heavy filling material.*

## GAUGE

*Gauge is not critical for this project. Ensure your stitches are tight so the stuffing won't show through.*

For more information on how to make Daniel, including tips, step-by-step pictures, and videos, scan this QR code!

## HEAD

With **Root Beer**.

**Rnd 1:** 6 sc in magic ring

**Rnd 2:** 6 inc [12]

**Rnd 3:** (1 sc, 1 inc) × 6 [18]

**Rnd 4:** 1 sc, 1 inc, (2 sc, 1 inc) × 5, 1 sc [24]

**Rnd 5:** (3 sc, 1 inc) × 6 [30]

**Rnd 6:** 2 sc, 1 inc, (4 sc, 1 inc) × 5, 2 sc [36]

**Rnd 7:** (5 sc, 1 inc) × 6 [42]

**Rnd 8:** 3 sc, 1 inc, (6 sc, 1 inc) × 5, 3 sc [48]

**Rnd 9:** (7 sc, 1 inc) × 6 [54]

**Rnds 10–22:** 54 sc (13 rounds)

Insert the eyes between rounds 17 and 18, with 9 sc visible apart from each other.

**Rnd 23:** (7 sc, 1 dec) × 6 [48]

**Rnd 24:** 2 sc, 1 dec, (4 sc, 1 dec) × 7, 2 sc [40]

**Rnd 25:** 1 sc, 1 dec, (2 sc, 1 dec) × 9, 1 sc [30]

**Rnd 26:** (1 sc, 1 dec) × 10 [20]

Stuff the Head until round 26. Do not stuff from round 27 on.

**Rnd 27:** Blo 20 sc

**Rnds 28–35:** 20 sc (8 rounds)

**Rnd 36:** 10 dec [10]

Fasten off with an inverted magic ring.

Push the neck inward (from round 27 to 36) with the help of the hook handle.

For more instructions, see page 167.

## EARS (MAKE 2)

With **Root Beer**.

**Rnd 1:** 1 sc, 4 hdc, 1 sc in magic ring

Finish off and leave a long tail.

## NOSE

With **Root Beer**.

**Rnd 1:** 6 sc in magic ring

**Rnd 2:** (2 sc, 1 inc) × 2 [8]

Leave a long tail.

## ROBE

With **Ultramarine**, make 36 chains and close them into a ring with 1 sc. This will be the first stitch of the round.

**Rnds 1–10:** 36 sc (10 rounds)

**Rnd 11:** 2 sc, 1 dec, (4 sc, 1 dec) × 5, 2 sc [30]

Don't fasten off, as we will continue crocheting it with the Body.

## LEFT LEG

With **Root Beer**.

We will work on both sides of the chains. Start with 5 chains and from the second chain from the hook make:

**Rnd 1:** 1 inc, 2 sc, in the last chain 4 sc, continue on the other side of the chains 2 sc, 1 inc [12]

**Rnd 2:** 2 inc, 2 sc, 4 inc, 2 sc, 2 inc [20]

**Rnd 3:** 20 BPsc

**Rnds 4–5:** 20 sc (2 rounds)

Fill the feet with a little weight (aquarium gravel, stones, or another clean heavy material) so the amigurumi can balance on its knees.

**Rnd 6:** 6 sc, 4 dec, 6 sc [16]

**Rnd 7:** 4 sc, 4 dec, 4 sc [12]

**Rnds 8–10:** 12 sc (3 rounds)

We will now work on making the knees.

**Note:** To create the curve on the knees, we are not increasing or decreasing stitches. Instead, we are moving the beginning of each round slightly to the right, and we do not crochet the complete round, which forces the fabric to bend.

Here is how it works:

Crochet the number of stitches indicated for the curve.

STOP after reaching the indicated number, even though you haven't gone all the way around.

Cut the yarn and fasten off.

To begin the next Curve, insert the hook 1 stitch to the right of where you had started the previous Curve.

Reattach the yarn and continue crocheting the next Curve.

Every time you shift the starting point by 1 stitch, the curve side becomes *longer*, and the opposite side becomes *shorter*.

Skip 5 sc and reattach the yarn in the sixth stitch of the round.

**Curve 1:** 3 hdc, fasten off, reattach yarn 1 st to the right

**Curve 2:** 5 hdc, fasten off, reattach yarn 1 st to the right

**Curve 3:** 7 hdc, fasten off, reattach yarn 1 st to the right

**Curve 4:** 9 hdc, fasten off, reattach yarn 1 st to the right

At this stage, we finish crocheting the Curve section, and we will continue crocheting the continuous rounds.

**Rnds 11–13:** 12 sc (3 rounds)

**Rnd 14:** Change to **Snow White**. 12 sc

Stuff the Leg and fasten off.

## RIGHT LEG

Repeat rounds 1 to 14 of the Left Leg.

Make **4 more sc** and **3 chains** to get to the side of the Leg.

## BODY

With **Snow White**, continue the Body by joining both Legs. Stuff the Body as you crochet.

**Note:** You can also insert craft wire inside the amigurumi, running from the tip of the feet to the waist. This will provide extra support and help the amigurumi stay firmly in a kneeling position.

**Rnd 15:** 12 sc, 3 sc on the chain, 12 sc, 3 sc on the chain [30]

**Rnds 16–21:** 30 sc (6 rounds)

Fasten off **Snow White**. Place the Robe on the Body. Crochet both pieces together with **Ultramarine**.

**Rnd 22:** 30 sc (joining the Body and the Robe)

**Rnd 23:** 30 sc

**Rnd 24:** (13 sc, 1 dec) × 2 [28]

**Rnd 25:** 28 sc

**Rnd 26:** 6 sc, 1 dec, 12 sc, 1 dec, 6 sc [26]

**Rnd 27:** 26 sc

**Rnd 28:** (11 sc, 1 dec) × 2 [24]

**Rnd 29:** 24 sc

**Rnd 30:** Flo 24 hdc

Fasten off.

Using the back loops of round 30, attach **Root Beer** and make:

**Rnd 30:** 24 sc

**Rnd 31:** 2 sc, 1 dec, (4 sc, 1 dec) × 3, 2 sc [20]

**Rnd 32:** (3 sc, 1 dec) × 4 [16]

**Rnds 33–38:** 16 sc (6 rounds)

**Rnd 39:** 8 dec [8]

Stuff the Body, stuff the neck firmly, fasten off, and leave a long tail to attach the Body and the Head.

## ARMS (MAKE 2)

With **Root Beer**.

**Rnd 1:** 6 sc in magic ring

**Rnd 2:** (2 sc, 1 inc) × 2 [8]

**Rnds 3–11:** 8 sc (9 rounds)

**Rnd 12:** (1 sc, 1 inc) × 4 [12]

Fasten off both pieces.

## SLEEVES (MAKE 2)

With **Ultramarine**. Make 18 chains and close them with 1 sc. This will be the first st of the round.

**Rnds 1–2:** 18 sc (2 rounds)

**Rnd 3:** 7 sc, 2 dec, 7 sc [16]

**Rnd 4:** 16 sc

**Rnd 5:** 6 sc, 2 dec, 6 sc [14]

**Rnd 6:** 14 sc

**Rnd 7:** 5 sc, 2 dec, 5 sc [12]

**Rnds 8–9:** 12 sc (2 rounds)

Insert the Arms inside the Sleeves. Crochet both pieces together.

**Rnd 10:** 12 sc joining the Arms and the Sleeves

**Rnd 11:** 12 sc

Pinch Arms opening closed and crochet together with 6 sc. Leave a long tail.

## HAIR

With **Jet Black**.

**Rnd 1:** 6 sc in magic ring
**Rnd 2:** 6 inc [12]
**Rnd 3:** (1 sc, 1 inc) × 6 [18]
**Rnd 4:** 1 sc, 1 inc, (2 sc, 1 inc) × 5, 1 sc [24]
**Rnd 5:** (3 sc, 1 inc) × 6 [30]
**Rnd 6:** 2 sc, 1 inc, (4 sc, 1 inc) × 5, 2 sc [36]
**Rnd 7:** (5 sc, 1 inc) × 6 [42]
**Rnd 8:** 3 sc, 1 inc, (6 sc, 1 inc) × 5, 3 sc [48]
**Rnd 9:** (7 sc, 1 inc) × 6 [54]
**Rnd 10:** 18 sc, 2 sl, 2 sc, 3 hdc, 4 dc, 3 hdc, 2 sc, 2 sl st, 18 sc [54]
From round 10 on we will work in rows.
**Row 11:** 18 sc, chain and turn
**Rows 12–13:** 36 sc, chain and turn (2 rounds)
**Rnd 14:** 1 dec, 32 sc, 1 dec, chain and turn [34]
**Rnd 15:** 34 sc
**Rnd 16:** 1 dec, 30 sc, 1 dec, chain and turn [32]
**Rnds 17–23:** 32 sc, chain and turn (7 rounds)
Now crochet around the Hair for a better finish.
Crochet 13 sc on the sides (where you crocheted rows).
On the front part of Hair, make: 2 sl st, 6 sc, 2 hdc, 6 sc, 2 sl st

## BELT

With **Ginger Gold**.

Make 52 chains and from the second chain from the hook make 51 sl st.
Fasten off.

## ASSEMBLY

Using a tapestry needle to attach the Head to the Body, pass the remaining tail of the Head and the remaining tail of the Body to the middle of the magic ring that started the Head.

Pull the two ends in order to adjust the Head to the Body, tie a knot and cut the tails. This way, the Head will be articulated.

**Note:** I advise you to pin all the parts before sewing.

Sew the Arms vertically on the side of the Body, between rounds 24 and 27. Observe that the Arms must make a praying position in front of the Body. Once they are well placed, you can apply a drop of glue to the hands to stick them together.

Place the Belt on the Body.

Sew the Ears between rounds 16 and 19 (same line as the eyes), 3 sc apart from the eyes.

Make the details on the outer corner of the eyes with **Snow White**, see page 164.

If you want the eyes to be indented, see page 164.

With **Jet Black**, make the eyebrows with their outer corner 1 round above the eyes and the inner corner 2 rounds above the eyes, with a width of 4 sc.

Sew the Nose between rounds 18 and 19, 3 sc distant from the eyes.

Place the Hair on the Head of your amigurumi.

# Lion

## YARN

Fingering weight (#1 super fine) yarn, shown in Scheepjes *Catona* (100% mercerized cotton, 174 yd. / 125 m per 1.75 oz. / 50 g ball)

**BODY**

179 Topaz

**MANE/MUZZLE**

507 Chocolate

**PAWS/MUZZLE**

505 Linen

Any standard black embroidery thread can be used for the crosses on the mouth.

## FINISHED MEASUREMENTS

**HEIGHT:** 5.5 in. / 14 cm

**WIDTH:** 3.9 in. / 10 cm

## HOOK

- US B-1 / 2.0 mm crochet hook
- US C-2 / 2.5 mm crochet hook for the Mane

***Note:*** *Everything is worked with US B-1 / 2.0 mm crochet hook except for the Mane.*

## NOTIONS

- Pair of 13 mm safety eyes
- Polyester stuffing
- Tapestry needle
- Removable stitch markers
- Sewing pins
- Pointy tweezers

## GAUGE

*Gauge is not critical for this project. Ensure your stitches are tight so the stuffing won't show through.*

For more information on how to make the Lion, including tips, step-by-step pictures, and videos, scan this QR code!

## HEAD

With **Topaz**.
**Rnd 1:** 6 sc in magic ring
**Rnd 2:** 6 inc [12]
**Rnd 3:** (1 sc, 1 inc) × 6 [18]
**Rnd 4:** 1 sc, 1 inc, (2 sc, 1 inc) × 5, 1 sc [24]
**Rnd 5:** (3 sc, 1 inc) × 6 [30]
**Rnd 6:** 2 sc, 1 inc, (4 sc, 1 inc) × 5, 2 sc [36]
**Rnd 7:** (5 sc, 1 inc) × 6 [42]
**Rnd 8:** 3 sc, 1 inc, (6 sc, 1 inc) × 5, 3 sc [48]
**Rnd 9:** (7 sc, 1 inc) × 6 [54]
**Rnd 10:** 4 sc, 1 inc, (8 sc, 1 inc) × 5, 4 sc [60]
**Rnds 11–23:** 60 sc (14 rounds)
Insert the eyes between rounds 16 and 17, 11 visible sc apart. Add stuffing as you close your piece.
**Rnd 24:** 4 sc, 1 dec, (8 sc, 1 dec) × 5, 4 sc [54]
**Rnd 25:** (7 sc, 1 dec) × 6 [48]
**Rnd 26:** 2 sc, 1 dec, (4 sc, 1 dec) × 7, 2 sc [40]
**Rnd 27:** (3 sc, 1 dec) × 8 [32]
**Rnd 28:** 1 sc, 1 dec, (2 sc, 1 dec) × 7, 1 sc [24]
**Rnd 29:** (1 sc, 1 dec) × 8 [16]
**Rnd 30:** 8 dec [8]
Close with an inverted magic ring and fasten off.

## FRONT LEGS (MAKE 2)

With **Linen**.
**Rnd 1:** 8 sc in magic ring
**Rnd 2:** 8 inc [16]
**Rnd 3:** 6 sc, 4 inc, 6 sc [20]
**Rnds 4–5:** 20 sc (2 rounds)
**Rnd 6:** 6 sc, 4 dec, 6 sc [16]
**Rnd 7:** Change to **Topaz**. 16 sc
**Rnds 8–14:** 16 sc (7 rounds)
Fasten off both Legs.

## HIND LEGS (MAKE 2)

With **Linen**.
**Rnd 1:** 8 sc in magic ring
**Rnd 2:** 8 inc [16]
**Rnd 3:** 6 sc, 4 inc, 6 sc [20]
**Rnds 4–5:** 20 sc (2 rounds)
**Rnd 6:** 6 sc, 4 dec, 6 sc [16]
**Rnd 7:** Change to **Topaz**. 16 sc
**Rnds 8–11:** 16 sc (4 rounds)
**Rnd 12:** 6 sc, 4 inc, 6 sc [20]
**Rnd 13:** 20 sc
**Rnd 14:** 9 sc, 2 inc, 9 sc [22]
Add stuffing up to **round 13** only. From **round 14** onward, leave the Legs unstuffed so they can be sewn to the Body.
**Rnds 15–17:** 22 sc (3 rounds)
**Rnd 18:** 9 sc, 2 dec, 9 sc [20]
**Rnd 19:** 6 sc, 4 dec, 6 sc [16]
**Rnd 20:** 4 sc, 4 dec, 4 sc [12]
**Rnd 21:** 6 dec [6]
Fasten off.

## BODY

With **Topaz**.
**Rnd 1:** 8 sc in magic ring
**Rnd 2:** 8 inc [16]
**Rnd 3:** (1 sc, 1 inc) × 8 [24]
**Rnd 4:** 1 sc, 1 inc, (2 sc, 1 inc) × 7, 1 sc [32]
**Rnd 5:** (3 sc, 1 inc) × 8 [40]
**Rnd 6:** 2 sc, 1 inc, (4 sc, 1 inc) × 7, 2 sc [48]
**Rnd 7:** 48 sc
**Rnd 8:** (7 sc, 1 inc) × 6 [54]
**Rnds 9–14:** 54 sc (6 rounds)
**Rnd 15:** (7 sc, 1 dec) × 6 [48]
**Rnd 16:** 48 sc
**Rnd 17:** 17 sc, 6 sc in the Leg, 2 sc, 6 sc in the Leg, 17 sc [48]
**Rnd 18:** 17 sc, 10 sc in the Leg, 2 sc, 10 sc in the Leg, 17 sc [56]
**Rnds 19–21:** 56 sc (3 rounds)
**Rnd 22:** (5 sc, 1 dec) × 8 [48]

**Rnds 23–24:** 48 sc (2 rounds)
**Rnd 25:** 2 sc, 1 dec, (4 sc, 1 dec) × 7, 2 sc [40]
**Rnd 26:** 40 sc
Leave a long tail.

## TAIL

With **Black Coffee**.
**Rnd 1:** 6 sc in magic ring
**Rnd 2:** Blo (1 sc, 1 inc) × 3 [9]
**Rnd 3:** Blo (2 sc, 1 inc) × 3 [12]
**Rnd 4:** Blo 12 sc
**Rnd 5:** Change to **Topaz** 12 sc
**Rnds 6–15:** 12 sc (10 rounds)
Stuff the tail as you go and leave a long tail.

## EARS (MAKE 2)

With **Topaz**.
**Rnd 1:** 6 sc in magic ring
**Rnd 2:** 6 inc [12]
**Rnd 3:** (1 sc, 1 inc) × 6 [18]
**Rnd 4:** 1 sc, 1 inc, (2 sc, 1 inc) × 5, 1 sc [24]
**Rnds 5–7:** 24 sc (3 rounds)
Leave a long tail.

## BACK PART OF THE MANE

With **Chocolate** and US C-2 / 2.5 mm hook make:
**Rnd 1:** 6 sc in magic ring
**Rnd 2:** Blo 6 inc [12]
**Rnd 3:** Blo (1 sc, 1 inc) × 6 [18]
**Rnd 4:** Blo 1 sc, 1 inc, (2 sc, 1 inc) × 5, 1 sc [24]
**Rnd 5:** Blo (3 sc, 1 inc) × 6 [30]
**Rnd 6:** Blo 2 sc, 1 inc, (4 sc, 1 inc) × 5, 2 sc [36]
**Rnd 7:** Blo (5 sc, 1 inc) × 6 [42]
**Rnd 8:** Blo 3 sc, 1 inc, (6 sc, 1 inc) × 5, 3 sc [48]
**Rnd 9:** Blo (7 sc, 1 inc) × 6 [54]
**Rnd 10:** Blo 4 sc, 1 inc, (8 sc, 1 inc) × 5, 4 sc [60]
**Rnds 11–14:** Blo 60 sc (4 rounds)
From this round on, we will work in rows, making a chain and turning the crochet piece.
**Row 15:** Blo 20 sc, chain and turn
**Row 16:** Flo 40 sc, chain and turn
**Row 17:** Blo 1 dec, 36 sc, 1 dec, chain and turn [38]
**Row 18:** Flo 1 dec, 34 sc, 1 dec, chain and turn [36]
**Row 19:** Blo 1 dec, 32 sc, 1 dec, chain and turn [34]

**Row 20:** Flo 34 sc, chain and turn
**Row 21:** Blo 34 sc, chain and turn
**Row 22:** Flo 34 sc, chain and turn
Fasten off.

To make the curls of the Mane, insert the crochet hook in the first loop from the top of the Mane (closer to the magic ring).
Make 3 chains and close them with 1 sl st in the following loop of the base. Make 1 sl st again and repeat the sequence, until you have all the loops worked on and a great volume on the Mane.

## FRONT PART OF THE MANE

With **Chocolate** and US C-2 / 2.5 mm hook make:
Make 56 chains and close them with 1 sc. This will be the first st of the round.
**Rnd 1:** 56 sc
Now make the curls of the Mane. Make 3 chains and close them with 1 sl st in the following st of the base. Make 1 sl st again and repeat the sequence.
**Note:** Make curls in both sides of this ring in order to give volume to the Mane.
When finishing one side of the ring, you can make one more chain to continue on the other side of the ring.

## MUZZLE

With **Linen**.
**Rnd 1:** 6 sc in magic ring
**Rnd 2:** (inc3sc, 1 sc) × 3 [12]
**Rnd 3:** 1 sc, inc3sc, (3 sc, inc3sc) × 2, 2 sc [18]
**Rnd 4:** 2 sc, inc3sc, (5 sc, inc3sc) × 2, 3 sc [24]
**Rnd 5:** 3 sc, inc3sc, 7 sc, inc3sc, 7 sc, Change to **Topaz** inc3sc, 4 sc [30]
**Rnds 6–8: Topaz:** 5 sc, **Linen:** 18 sc, **Topaz:** 7 sc [30]
**Rnd 9: Topaz:** 5 sc
Leave a long tail.
**Note:** Inc3sc means you need to crochet 3 sc together in the same stitch.

## ASSEMBLY

**Note:** Using pins when sewing is an extremely important part of the process. Make sure all parts are pinned and well placed before fastening off.
Sew the Head to the Body, aligning the eyes with the Front Legs.
Sew the Hind Legs on the side of the Body. Position the Body on a firm base like a table, just to make sure both

Legs are stable and touching the base. Sew them between rounds 7 and 14.

Sew the Tail in the back of the Body, between rounds 9 and 12. It should also help stabilize the Lion on a flat base.

Embroider the Muzzle with **Chocolate**. Work a triangle from the magic ring to the sides of the triangle. Once you outline the edges of the triangle, pass the yarn several times horizontally to fill the space inside the triangle.

Starting at the magic ring, pass the yarn 5 sc upward to form a triangle, working from the center toward each side of the color change. Make sure the top edge of the triangle is between rounds 5 and 6, reaching from one side of the color change to the other, so the Muzzle looks centered on the face.

Once the triangle outline is complete, pass the yarn back and forth horizontally inside the shape to fill it in, keeping the lines close together for a solid finish.

Sew the Nose between rounds 16 and 25.

With **Chocolate**, make the eyebrows with their outer corner 1 round above the eyes and the inner corner 2 rounds above the eyes, with a width of 4 sc.

Make the details on the outer corner of the eyes with **Snow White**, see page 164.

If you want the eyes to be indented, see page 164.

Embroider the details on the paws, making 3 vertical lines in the front part, between rounds 3 and 5.

Position the Back Part of the Mane with pins.

Pin the Front Part of the Mane in a way that it reaches the edges of the face and meets the Back Part, to ensure the continuity of the Mane.

Pin the Ears on top of the Back Part of the Mane. Since there is so much volume on the Mane, it is hard to determine the exact place for sewing.

**Note:** I advise you to pin the Ears and gently remove the Back Part of Mane. Sew the Ears in the attached position.

After that, glue both sides of the Mane to the Head.

Sew a few crosses in the Lion's Muzzle with **Black** embroidery thread, so that it looks like its mouth is sealed.

# The Story of Joseph and His Coat of Many Colors

Genesis 37–50

**Joseph, the favorite son of Jacob, has one of the most intriguing stories in the Bible. After being gifted a glorious coat of many colors by his father, Joseph's ten older brothers flew into a fit of jealousy; and when Joseph shared dreams of ruling over his brothers, their jealousy turned into rage. The brothers decided to get rid of him by selling him into Egyptian slavery, and tricking their father into believing he was dead. Despite years of hardship and wrongful imprisonment, Joseph kept his integrity; and his ability to interpret dreams allowed him to rise in the ranks to become the second most powerful man in Egypt. After predicting—and saving Egypt from—a famine, he used his position to save his family from starving. Joseph's brothers come to see him:**

> And his brethren also went and fell down before his face; and they said, Behold,
> we be thy servants.[18] And Joseph said unto them, Fear not: for am I in the place
> of God?[19] But as for you, ye thought evil against me; but God meant it unto good,
> to bring to pass, as it is this day, to save much people alive.[20] Now therefore fear
> ye not: I will nourish you, and your little ones. And he comforted them, and spake
> kindly unto them.[21] And Joseph dwelt in Egypt, he, and his father's house: and
> Joseph lived an hundred and ten years.[22]

**—Genesis 50:18–22**

Despite the betrayal of his brothers, Joseph's choice to forgive them shows us that even in the face of hatred, it is possible to live with forgiveness and integrity.

# Joseph

## YARN

Fingering weight (#1 super fine) yarn, shown in Scheepjes *Catona* (100% mercerized cotton, 174 yd. / 125 m per 1.75 oz. / 50 g ball)

**SKIN**

255 Shell

**SHOES**

162 Black Coffee

**HAIR**

157 Root Beer

**EYE DETAIL**

106 Snow White

**OUTFIT**

130 Old Lace

**BELT**

383 Ginger Gold

**VEST**

115 Hot Red

253 Tropic

384 Powder Blue

208 Yellow Gold

## FINISHED MEASUREMENTS

**HEIGHT:** 5.5 in. / 14 cm
**WIDTH:** 3.15 in. / 8 cm

## HOOK

- US B-1 / 2.0 mm crochet hook for the Body
- US C-2 / 2.5 mm crochet hook for the Hair

*Note: Everything is worked with US B-1 / 2.0 mm crochet hook except for the Hair.*

## NOTIONS

- Pair of 13 mm safety eyes
- Polyester stuffing
- Tapestry needle
- Removable stitch markers
- Sewing pins
- Pointy tweezers
- Craft glue

## GAUGE

*Gauge is not critical for this project. Ensure your stitches are tight so the stuffing won't show through.*

For more information on how to make Joseph, including tips, step-by-step pictures, and videos, scan this QR code!

## HEAD

With **Shell**.

**Rnd 1:** 6 sc in magic ring
**Rnd 2:** 6 inc [12]
**Rnd 3:** (1 sc, 1 inc) × 6 [18]
**Rnd 4:** 1 sc, 1 inc, (2 sc, 1 inc) × 5, 1 sc [24]
**Rnd 5:** (3 sc, 1 inc) × 6 [30]
**Rnd 6:** 2 sc, 1 inc, (4 sc, 1 inc) × 5, 2 sc [36]
**Rnd 7:** (5 sc, 1 inc) × 6 [42]
**Rnd 8:** 3 sc, 1 inc, (6 sc, 1 inc) × 5, 3 sc [48]
**Rnd 9:** 48 sc
**Rnd 10:** (5 sc, 1 inc) × 8 [56]
**Rnds 11–22:** 56 sc (12 rounds)
Insert the eyes between rounds 17 and 18, with 8 sc visible apart from each other.
**Rnd 23:** (5 sc, 1 dec) × 8 [48]
**Rnd 24:** 2 sc, 1 dec, (4 sc, 1 dec) × 7, 2 sc [40]
**Rnd 25:** 1 sc, 1 dec, (2 sc, 1 dec) × 9, 1 sc [30]
**Rnd 26:** (1 sc, 1 dec) × 10 [20]
Stuff the Head until round 26. Do not stuff from round 27 on.
**Rnd 27:** Blo 20 sc
**Rnds 28–35:** 20 sc (8 rounds)
**Rnd 36:** 10 dec [10]
Fasten off with an inverted magic ring.
Push the neck inward (from round 27 to 36) with the help of the hook handle.
For more instructions, see page 167.

## EARS (MAKE 2)

With **Shell**.

**Rnd 1:** 1 sc, 4 hdc, 1 sc in magic ring
Finish off and leave a long tail to sew.

## NOSE

With **Shell**.

Embroider the Nose between **rounds 18** and **19**, leaving **3 sc** away from the eyes. Pass the yarn horizontally **2 times** at a distance of **2 sc**. Then, pass the same yarn several times vertically and fasten off.

## EYEBROWS (MAKE 2)

With **Root Beer**, make the Eyebrows with their outer corner 1 round above the eyes and the inner corner 2 rounds above the eyes, with a width of 4 sc.

## ROBE

With **Old Lace**, make 32 chains and close them into a ring with 1 sc. This will be the first stitch of the round.

**Rnds 1–3:** 32 sc (3 rounds)
**Rnd 4:** 7 sc, 1 dec, 14 sc, 1 dec, 7 sc [30]
**Rnds 5–7:** 30 sc (3 rounds)
**Rnd 8:** (13 sc, 1 dec) × 2 [28]
**Rnds 9–11:** 28 sc (3 rounds)
Don't fasten off, as we will continue crocheting with **Old Lace** for the Body.

## LEFT LEG

With **Black Coffee**.

We will work on both sides of the chains. Start with 5 chains and from the second chain from the hook make:

**Rnd 1:** 1 inc, 2 sc, in the last chain 4 sc, continue on the other side of the chains 2 sc, 1 inc [12]
**Rnd 2:** 2 inc, 2 sc, 4 inc, 2 sc, 2 inc [20]
**Rnd 3:** 20 BPsc
**Rnd 4:** 20 sc
**Rnd 5:** Change to **Shell**. Blo 20 sl st
**Rnd 6:** Insert the hook below both loops of the slip stitch. 20 sc
**Rnd 7:** 6 sc, 4 dec, 6 sc [16]
**Rnd 8:** 4 sc, 4 dec, 4 sc [12]
**Rnds 9–13:** 12 sc (5 rounds)
**Rnd 14:** Change to **Old Lace**. 12 sc
Stuff the Leg and fasten off.
If you want your amigurumi to have flat feet to stand, make sure that you don't stuff it too much and leave it concave.

## RIGHT LEG

Repeat rounds 1 to 14 of the Left Leg.
Make **4 more sc** and **2 chains** to get to the side of the Leg.

## BODY

With **Old Lace**, we will continue the Body by joining both Legs. Be sure that both feet are facing forward at the junction of the Legs. Stuff the Body as you crochet.

**Rnd 15:** 12 sc, 2 sc on the chain, 12 sc, 2 sc on the chain [28]
**Rnds 16–21:** 28 sc (6 rounds)
Fasten off **Old Lace**. Attach the Robe to the Body. Crochet both pieces together with **Old Lace**.

**Rnd 22:** 28 sc (joining the Body and the Robe)
**Rnd 23:** 28 sc
**Rnd 24:** 6 sc, 1 dec, 12 sc, 1 dec, 6 sc [26]
**Rnd 25:** 26 sc
**Rnd 26:** (11 sc, 1 dec) × 2 [24]
**Rnds 27–28:** 24 sc (2 rounds)
**Rnd 29:** Flo 24 hdc
Fasten off.
Using the back loops of round 29, attach **Shell** and make:
**Rnd 29:** 24 sc
**Rnd 30:** 2 sc, 1 dec, (4 sc, 1 dec) × 3, 2 sc [20]
**Rnd 31:** (3 sc, 1 dec) × 4 [16]
**Rnds 32–38:** 16 sc (7 rounds)
**Rnd 39:** 8 dec [8]
Stuff the Body, fasten off, and leave a long tail to attach the Body and the Head.

## SANDALS (MAKE 2)

With **Black Coffee**. Make 10 chains, and from the second chain from the hook make 8 hdc.
Leave a long tail.

## ARMS (MAKE 2)

With **Shell**.
**Rnd 1:** 6 sc in magic ring
**Rnd 2:** (2 sc, 1 inc) × 2 [8]
**Rnd 3:** 8 sc
**Rnd 4:** Change to **Old Lace**. 8 sc
**Rnds 5–9:** 8 sc (5 rounds)
Slightly stuff half of the Arms (until round 4).
Pinch Arm opening closed and crochet together with 4 sc. Leave a long tail.

### HAIR (PART I)

With **Root Beer**. **Note:** The Hair is crocheted in 3 parts.

**Rnd 1:** 6 sc in magic ring

**Rnd 3:** Flo (1 sc, 1 inc) × 6 [18]

**Rnd 4:** 1 sc, 1 inc, (2 sc, 1 inc) × 5, 1 sc [24]

**Rnd 5:** (3 sc, 1 inc) × 6 [30]

**Rnd 6:** 2 sc, 1 inc, (4 sc, 1 inc) × 5, 2 sc [36]

Now we will work around the 36 sc of round 6 to make the Hair strands.

**Strnd 1:** 10 chains, and from the third chain make 8 hdc, sl st in the next st.

**Strnds 2–17:** 19 chains, and from the third chain make 17 hdc, sc in the next st. (18 strands)

**Strnd 18:** 10 chains, and from the third chain make 8 hdc, sl st in the next st.

Fasten off.

### HAIR (PART II)

Position the Hair with the "wrong" side of the magic ring up. Insert the crochet hook in the first st next to the strand of Hair Part I.

Make 8 chains, and from the third chain make 6 hdc, sl st in the next st. Sl st in the following st and restart the sequence.

Repeat 8 times and fasten off.

### HAIR (PART III)

Using the Front loops of Part I of the Hair, on round 3, make:

**Strnds 1–12:** 12 chains, and from the third chain make 10 hdc, sl st in the next st. Fasten off.

## VEST

With **Hot Red**, make 21 chains and from the second chain from the hook:

**Note:** Do not make chains to turn the piece.

**Row 1:** 20 sc, turn

**Row 2:** 2 sc, inc3, 3 sc, inc3, 6 sc, inc3, 3 sc, inc3, 2 sc, turn [28]

**Row 3:** Change to **Yellow Gold**. 3 sc, inc3, 5 sc, inc3, 8 sc, inc3, 5 sc, inc3, 3 sc, turn [36]

**Row 4:** 4 sc, inc3, 7 sc, inc3, 10 sc, inc3, 7 sc, inc3, 4 sc, turn [44]

**Row 5:** Change to **Powder Blue**. 5 sc. inc3, 9 sc, inc3, 12 sc, inc3, 9 sc, inc3, 5 sc, turn [52]

**Row 6:** 7 sc, 5 chains and skip 11 sc, 16 sc, 5 chains and skip 11 sc, 7 sc, turn [40]

**Row 7:** Change to **Tropic**. 40 sc, turn

**Row 8:** 9 sc, 1 dec, 18 sc, 1 dec, 9 sc, turn [38]

**Rows 9–10: Hot Red**. 38 sc, turn (2 rows)

**Rows 11–12: Yellow Gold**. 38 sc, turn (2 rows)

**Rows 13–14: Powder Blue**. 38 sc, turn (2 rows)

**Rows 15–16: Tropic**. 38 sc, turn (2 rows)

**Rows 17–18: Hot Red:** 38 sc, turn (2 rows)

Now we will crochet around the Vest with **Hot Red**.

On one side, make 16 sc, 1 inc hdc, 1 inc dc.

On the top part of the Vest (the collar), crochet 20 hdc on the back loop.

On the other side, make 1 inc dc, 1 inc hdc, 16 sc.

Fasten off.

## SLEEVES (MAKE 2)

With **Powder Blue**, attach the yarn in the hole created in round 6 of the Vest and make:

**Rnd 1:** 18 sc

**Rnd 2:** Change to **Tropic**. 18 sc

**Rnd 3:** 4 sc, 1 inc, 8 sc, 1 inc, 4 sc [20]

**Rnd 4:** Change to **Hot Red**. (9 sc, 1 inc) × 2 [22]

**Rnd 5:** 22 sc

Fasten off.

## BELT

With **Ginger Gold**.

Make 52 chains and from the second chain from the hook make 51 sl st.

Fasten off.

## ASSEMBLY

Using a tapestry needle to attach the Head to the Body, pass the remaining tail of the Head and the remaining tail of the Body to the middle of the magic ring that started the Head.

Pull the two ends in order to adjust the Head to the Body, tie a knot and cut the tails. This way, the Head will be articulated.

Sew the Arms between rounds 25 and 26, on the side of the Body, with 9 sc distant in the front part of the Body.

Attach the Belt to the amigurumi.

Attach the Straps of the Sandals to the front part of the feet.

Attach the Vest to the amigurumi. Sew the Ears between rounds 16 and 18 (same line as the eyes), 3 sc apart from the eyes.

Make the details on the outer corner of the eyes with **Snow White**, see page 164.

If you want the eyes to be indented, see page 164.

**Note:** I advise pinning every strand of Hair before applying glue. Just a drop of glue in each strand of Hair should be enough to fix it.

Place the Hair on the Head.

Pin strands 1 and 18 above the Ears.

Pin strands 2 to 17 around the Head, behind the Ears.

Pin the strands of Part II of the Hair in Joseph's forehead.

Distribute evenly the strands of Hair created in Part III on the top of the Head.

# The Story of Jonah and the Whale

Jonah 1–2

**When the Lord commanded the prophet Jonah to preach to the wicked city of Nineveh, Jonah, fearing the Lord, fled on a ship sailing in the opposite direction. But the Lord sent a ferocious storm that soon overtook the ship. Jonah, recognizing this was God's punishment, threw himself overboard in an attempt to save his shipmates' lives. Our amigurumis illustrate the next part of the story:**

> Now the Lord had prepared a great fish to swallow up Jonah. And Jonah was in the belly of the fish three days and three nights.[17]
>
> Then Jonah prayed unto the Lord his God out of the fish's belly[1] And said, I cried by reason of mine affliction unto the Lord, and he heard me; out of the belly of hell cried I, and thou heardest my voice.[2] For thou hadst cast me into the deep, in the midst of the seas; and the floods compassed me about: all thy billows and thy waves passed over me.[3] Then I said, I am cast out of thy sight; yet I will look again toward thy holy temple.[4] The waters compassed me about, even to the soul: the depth closed me round about, the weeds were wrapped about my head.[5] I went down to the bottoms of the mountains; the earth with her bars was about me for ever: yet hast thou brought up my life from corruption, O Lord my God.[6] When my soul fainted within me I remembered the Lord: and my prayer came in unto thee, into thine holy temple.[7] They that observe lying vanities forsake their own mercy.[8] But I will sacrifice unto thee with the voice of thanksgiving; I will pay that that I have vowed. Salvation is of the Lord.[9] And the Lord spake unto the fish, and it vomited out Jonah upon the dry land.[10]

**—Jonah 1:17, 2:1–10**

Jonah's journey teaches us that you cannot run away from responsibilities, and that repentance can lead to forgiveness and second chances—things we all need from time to time.

# Jonah

## YARN

Fingering weight (#1 super fine) yarn, shown in Scheepjes *Catona* (100% mercerized cotton, 174 yd. / 125 m per 1.75 oz. / 50 g ball)

**SKIN**

255 Shell

**HAIR/SHOES**

162 Black Coffee

**EYE DETAIL**

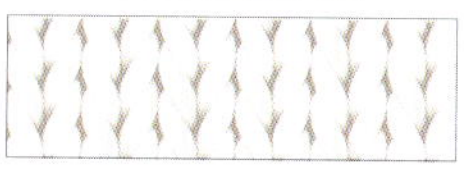

106 Snow White

**PANTS**

506 Caramel

**SHIRT**

505 Linen

Fingering weight (#1 super fine) yarn, shown in Hobbii *Friends Cotton 8/4* (100% cotton, 174 yd. / 160 m per 1.75 oz. / 50 g ball)

**BELT**

13 Ochre

Any standard brown embroidery thread can be used for the eyebrows.

## FINISHED MEASUREMENTS

**HEIGHT:** 5.5 in. / 14 cm
**WIDTH:** 2.75 in. / 7 cm

## HOOK

- US B-1 / 2.0 mm crochet hook for the Body
- US C-2 / 2.5 mm crochet hook for the Hair

*Note: Everything is worked with US B-1 / 2.0 mm crochet hook except for the Hair.*

## NOTIONS

- Pair of 13 mm safety eyes
- Polyester stuffing
- Tapestry needle
- Removable stitch markers
- Sewing pins
- Pointy tweezers
- Craft glue

## GAUGE

*Gauge is not critical for this project. Ensure your stitches are tight so the stuffing won't show through.*

For more information on how to make Jonah, including tips, step-by-step pictures, and videos, scan this QR code!

## HEAD

With **Shell**.

**Rnd 1:** 6 sc in magic ring
**Rnd 2:** 6 inc [12]
**Rnd 3:** (1 sc, 1 inc) × 6 [18]
**Rnd 4:** 1 sc, 1 inc, (2 sc, 1 inc) × 5, 1 sc [24]
**Rnd 5:** (3 sc, 1 inc) × 6 [30]
**Rnd 6:** 2 sc, 1 inc, (4 sc, 1 inc) × 5, 2 sc [36]
**Rnd 7:** (5 sc, 1 inc) × 6 [42]
**Rnd 8:** 3 sc, 1 inc, (6 sc, 1 inc) × 5, 3 sc [48]
**Rnd 9:** 48 sc
**Rnd 10:** (5 sc, 1 inc) × 8 [56]
**Rnds 11–22:** 56 sc (12 rounds)
Insert the eyes between rounds 17 and 18, with 7 sc visible apart from each other.
**Rnd 23:** (5 sc, 1 dec) × 8 [48]
**Rnd 24:** 2 sc, 1 dec, (4 sc, 1 dec) × 7, 2 sc [40]
**Rnd 25:** 1 sc, 1 dec, (2 sc, 1 dec) × 9, 1 sc [30]
**Rnd 26:** (1 sc, 1 dec) × 10 [20]
Stuff the Head until round 26. You should not stuff from round 27 on.
**Rnd 27:** Blo 20 sc
**Rnds 28–35:** 20 sc (8 rounds)
**Rnd 36:** 10 dec [10]
Fasten off with an inverted magic ring.
Push the neck inward (from round 27 to 36) with the help of the hook handle.
For more instructions, see page 167.

## EARS (MAKE 2)

With **Shell**, make a magic ring.
**Rnd 1:** In ring: 1 sc, 4 hdc, 1 sc
Finish off and leave a long tail.

## NOSE

With **Shell**.
Embroider the Nose between **rounds 18** and **19**, leaving **2 sc** away from the eyes. Pass the thread horizontally **4 times** at a distance of **3 sc**. Then, pass the same thread several times vertically and fasten off.

## EYEBROWS (MAKE 2)

With **Brown** embroidery thread, make the Eyebrows with the outer corner 1 round above the eyes and the inner corner 2 rounds above the eyes, with a width of 4 sc.

## PANTS

With **Caramel**, make 16 chains and close them into a ring with 1 sc. This will be the first stitch of the round.
**Rnd 1:** (1 sc, 1 inc) × 8 [24]
**Rnds 2–4:** 24 sc (3 rounds)
**Rnd 5:** (1 sc, 1 dec) × 8 [16]
**Rnd 6:** 16 sc
Fasten off the first Pant Leg and make the second Pant Leg from rounds 1 to 6. After you finish rnd 6, make 2 chains and attach to the first Pant Leg with 1 sc. This will be first st of the round.
**Rnd 7:** 16 sc, 2 sc in one side of the chains, 16 sc, 2 sc on the other side of the chains [36]
Do not fasten off! Set them aside, to be crocheted later on with the Body.

## LEFT LEG

With **Black Coffee**.
Work on both sides of the chain. Start with 5 chains and from the second chain from the hook make:
**Rnd 1:** 1 inc, 2 sc, in the last chain 4 sc, continue on the other side of the chains 2 sc, 1 inc [12]

**Rnd 2:** 2 inc, 2 sc, 4 inc, 2 sc, 2 inc [20]
**Rnd 3:** 20 BPsc
**Rnd 4:** 20 sc
**Rnd 5:** Change to **Shell**. Blo 20 sl st
**Rnd 6:** Insert the hook below both loops of the slip stitch. 20 sc
**Rnd 7:** 6 sc, 4 dec, 6 sc [16]
**Rnd 8:** 5 sc, 3 dec, 5 sc [13]
**Rnds 9–15:** 13 sc (7 rounds)
Stuff the Leg and fasten off.
If you want your amigurumi to have flat feet to stand, make sure that you don't stuff it too much and leave it concave.

## RIGHT LEG

Repeat rounds 1 to 15 of the Left Leg.
Make **4 more sc** and **2 chains** to get to the side of the Leg.
Place the Pants on the Body before joining the Legs.

## BODY

We will continue the Body by joining both Legs. Be sure that both feet are facing forward at the junction of the Legs. Stuff the Body as you crochet.
**Rnd 16:** 13 sc, 2 sc on the chain, 13 sc, 2 sc on the chain [30]
**Rnds 17–19:** 30 sc (3 rounds)
Fasten off.

### Continue working the Pants

With **Caramel**.
**Rnds 8–9:** 36 sc (2 rounds)
**Rnd 10:** (4 sc, 1 dec) × 6 [30]

Now we get back to crocheting the Pants together with the Body, with **Caramel**.

**Rnd 20:** 30 sc (joining both pieces)

**Rnd 21:** (13 sc, 1 dec) × 2 [28]

**Rnd 22:** 28 sc

**Rnd 23:** Change to **Linen**. Blo 28 sl st

**Rnd 24:** Blo 28 sc

**Rnd 25:** 6 sc, 1 dec, 12 sc, 1 dec, 6 sc [26]

**Rnd 26:** 26 sc

**Rnd 27:** (11 sc, 1 dec) × 2 [24]

**Rnds 28–29:** 24 sc (2 rounds)

**Rnd 30:** Flo 10 sc, inc3hdc, 1 chain, 2 sl st, 1 chain, inc3hdc, 10 sc

**Note:** Depending on your crochet tension, you may need to adjust the number of stitches at the beginning of this round. It is important to keep the inc3hdc, 1 ch, 2 sl st, 1 ch, inc3hdc centered, so the collar stays well aligned.

Fasten off the **Linen** color.

Using the back loops of round 30, attach **Shell** and make:

**Rnd 30:** 24 sc

**Rnd 31:** 2 sc, 1 dec, (4 sc, 1 dec) × 3, 2 sc [20]

**Rnd 32:** (8 sc, 1 dec) × 2 [18]

**Rnds 33–39:** 18 sc (7 rounds)

**Rnd 40:** 9 dec [9]

Stuff the Body, fasten off, and leave a long tail to attach the Body and the Head.

## SHIRT

With **Linen**. Place the Body upside down, and insert the crochet hook on the last loop of round 23. Crochet on the front loops of round 23.

**Rnd 1:** 3 sc, 1 inc, (6 sc, 1 inc) × 3, 3 sc [32]
**Rnd 2:** 32 sc
Fasten off.

## ARMS (MAKE 2)

With **Shell**.
**Rnd 1:** 6 sc in magic ring
**Rnd 2:** (2 sc, 1 inc) × 2 [8]
**Rnds 3–4:** 8 sc (2 rounds)
**Rnd 5:** Change to **Linen**. Blo 8 sl st
**Rnd 6:** Blo 8 sc
**Rnds 7–10:** 8 sc (4 rounds)
Slightly stuff half of the Arms (until round 5).
Pinch the Arms closed with 4 sc.
Fasten off and leave a long tail.

## HAIR (PART I)

We will crochet the Hair in two parts.
With **Black Coffee** and US C-2 / 2.55 mm hook.
**Rnd 1:** 6 sc in magic ring
**Rnd 2:** 6 inc [12]
**Rnd 3:** (1 sc, 1 inc) × 6 [18]
**Rnd 4:** 1 sc, 1 inc, (2 sc, 1 inc) × 5, 1 sc [24]
**Rnd 5:** (3 sc, 1 inc) × 6 [30]
**Rnd 6:** 2 sc, 1 inc, (4 sc, 1 inc) × 5, 2 sc [36]
**Rnd 7:** (5 sc, 1 inc) × 6 [42]
**Rnd 8:** 3 sc, 1 inc, (6 sc, 1 inc) × 5, 3 sc [48]
Now we will crochet the strands of Hair. Observe that you have 1 sl st between each strand of Hair.
**Strnd 1:** 10 chains, and from the third chain from the hook make 8 hdc. Close the strand of Hair with 1 sl st in the following st. 1 sl st in the next st.
**Strnds 2–17:** 18 chains, and from the third chain from the hook make 16 hdc. Close the strand of Hair with 1 sl st in the following st. 1 sl st in the next st.
**Strnd 18:** 10 chains, and from the third chain from the hook make 8 hdc. Close the strand of Hair with 1 sl st in the following st.
Fasten off.

## HAIR (PART II)

With **Black Coffee.**

We will crochet an oval piece from the foundation chain, by working on both sides of the chains.

Make 12 chains, and from the second chain from the hook, make:

**Rnd 1:** 11 sl st, 1 chain, 1 sl st (in the last stitch), continue in the other side of the chains, 10 sl st, 1 chain.

Sl st in the first st of the round. We will work around the oval piece to crochet the strands of Hair.

**Strnds 1–12:** 20 chains, and from the third chain from the hook make 18 hdc. Close the strand of Hair with 1 sl st in the following st. 1 sl st in the next st.

Fasten off.

## SANDALS

With **Black Coffee**.

Attach the yarn to the 5th loop created by round 5. Make 7 chains, skip 9 loops, and attach the chains with 1 slip stitch. Fasten off.

## BELT

With **Ochre**, make 52 chains and fasten off.

## ASSEMBLY

Using a tapestry needle to attach the Head to the Body, pass the remaining tail of the Head and the remaining tail of the Body to the middle of the magic ring that started the Head.

Pull the two ends in order to adjust the Head to the Body, tie a knot and cut the tails. This way, the Head will be articulated.

Sew the Arms between rounds 28 and 29, on the side of the Body, with 9 sc distant in the front part of the Body.

Tie the Belt around the Body, between the Shirt and the Pants.

Sew the Ears between rounds 16 and 18 (same line as the eyes), 3 sc apart from the eyes.

Make the details on the outer corner of the eyes with **Snow White**, see page 164.

If you want the eyes to be indented, see page 164.

**Note:** I always advise pinning every strand of Hair before applying glue. Just a drop of glue in each strand of Hair should be enough to fix it.

Place Part I of the Hair on the Head of your amigurumi, with the opposite side of the magic ring up. Strands 1 and 18 should be above the Ears. Place the remaining strands around the Head.

Part II of the Hair should be on the top of Part I.

Split the Hair to have 6 strands for the right side and 6 strands for the left side.

# *Whale*

## YARN

Fingering weight (#1 super fine) yarn, shown in Scheepjes *Catona* (100% mercerized cotton, 174 yd. / 125 m per 1.75 oz. / 50 g ball)

**BODY**

401 Dark Teal

**BELLY**

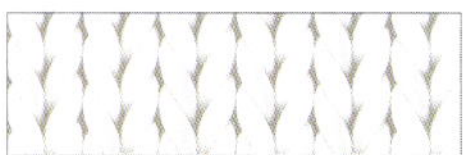

106 Snow White

## FINISHED MEASUREMENTS

**HEIGHT:** 8.3 in. / 21 cm

**WIDTH:** 7.9 in. / 20 cm

## HOOK

- US B-1 / 2.0 mm crochet hook

## NOTIONS

- Pair of 14 mm safety eyes
- Polyester stuffing
- Tapestry needle
- Removable stitch markers
- Sewing pins
- Pointy tweezers

## GAUGE

*Gauge is not critical for this project. Ensure your stitches are tight so the stuffing won't show through.*

For more information on how to make the Whale, including tips, step-by-step pictures, and videos, scan this QR code!

## BODY

With **Dark Teal**.

**Rnd 1:** 6 sc in magic ring
**Rnd 2:** 6 inc [12]
**Rnd 3:** 12 sc
**Rnd 4:** (1 sc, 1 inc) × 6 [18]
**Rnd 5:** 1 sc, 1 inc, (2 sc, 1 inc) × 5, 1 sc [24]
**Rnd 6:** (3 sc, 1 inc) × 6 [30]
**Rnd 7:** 2 sc, 1 inc, (4 sc, 1 inc) × 5, 2 sc [36]
**Rnd 8:** (5 sc, 1 inc) × 6 [42]
**Rnd 9:** 3 sc, 1 inc, (6 sc, 1 inc) × 5, 3 sc [48]
**Rnd 10:** (7 sc, 1 inc) × 6 [54]
**Rnd 11:** 4 sc, 1 inc, (8 sc, 1 inc) × 5, 4 sc [60]
**Rnd 12:** (9 sc, 1 inc) × 6 [66]
**Rnd 13:** 5 sc, 1 inc, (10 sc, 1 inc) × 5, 5 sc [72]
**Rnd 14:** (11 sc, 1 inc) × 6 [78]
**Rnd 15:** 6 sc, 1 inc, (12 sc, 1 inc) × 5, 6 sc [84]
**Rnd 16:** (13 sc, 1 inc) × 6 [90]
**Rnds 17–31:** 90 sc (15 rounds)
**Rnd 32:** 30 sc, (3 sc, 1 dec) × 6, 30 sc [84]
**Rnd 33:** 84 sc
**Rnd 34:** 27 sc, (3 sc, 1 dec) × 6, 27 sc [78]
**Rnd 35:** 78 sc
**Rnd 36:** 21 sc, (1 dec, 4 sc) × 6, 21 sc [72]
**Rnd 37:** 72 sc

**Rnd 38:** 21 sc, (3 sc, 1 dec) × 6, 21 sc [66]
**Rnd 39:** 66 sc
**Rnd 40:** 15 sc, (1 dec, 4 sc) × 6, 15 sc [60]
**Rnd 41:** 60 sc
Insert the eyes between rounds 20 and 21, with 45 sc distant from each other. Observe that the flat part of the Whale should be at the bottom of the piece, and the curved part should be up. Look at the Whale from the front (where you started the magic ring), to check if the eyes are evenly placed, before attaching the washer. Stuff the amigurumi as you crochet.
**Note:** Pay close attention to the stuffing while working on the Body. Add fiberfill gradually and shape it as you go, especially around the Whale's face. The face and the end of the Tail are two key areas that need extra care. If these parts are under-shaped, the face may look too flat. Take your time to adjust the stuffing to keep the curves soft and well defined.
**Rnd 42:** 12 sc, (4 sc, 1 dec) × 6, 12 sc [54]
**Rnd 43:** 54 sc
**Rnd 44:** 12 sc (1 dec, 3 sc) × 6, 12 sc [48]
**Rnd 45:** 48 sc
**Rnd 46:** 9 sc (3 sc, 1 dec) × 6, 9 sc [42]
**Rnds 47–50:** 42 sc (4 rounds)
**Rnd 51:** 37 sc
Round 51 ends with 37 sc. The following st you crochet will be the first st of the **curved section**.

**Note:** To create the curve in the Tail, you are not increasing or decreasing stitches. Instead, you are moving the beginning of each round slightly to the right and NOT crocheting the complete round, which will force the fabric to bend.

Here is how it works:
Crochet the number of stitches indicated for the Curve (for example: 12 sc).
STOP after reaching the indicated number, even though you haven't gone all the way around.
Cut the yarn and fasten off.

To begin the next Curve, insert the hook 1 stitch to the right of where you had started the previous Curve.

Reattach the yarn and continue crocheting the next Curve.

Every time you shift the starting point by 1 stitch, the curved side becomes *longer*, and the opposite side becomes *shorter*.

**Curve 1:** 12 sc, fasten off, reattach yarn 1 st to the right

**Curve 2:** 14 sc, fasten off, reattach yarn 1 st to the right

**Curve 3:** 16 sc, fasten off, reattach yarn 1 st to the right

**Curve 4:** 18 sc, fasten off, reattach yarn 1 st to the right

**Curve 5:** 20 sc, fasten off, reattach yarn 1 st to the right

**Curve 6:** 22 sc, fasten off, reattach yarn 1 st to the right

**Curve 7:** 24 sc, fasten off, reattach yarn 1 st to the right

**Curve 8:** 26 sc, fasten off, reattach yarn 1 st to the right

At this stage, continue crocheting in continuous rounds.

**Rnd 52:** 28 sc, and continue crocheting 14 sc to complete this round [42]

**Rnds 53–54:** 42 sc (2 rounds)

**Rnd 55:** (5 sc, 1 dec) × 6 [36]

**Rnds 56–61:** 36 (6 rounds)

**Rnd 62:** (4 sc, 1 dec) × 6 [30]

**Rnds 63–66:** 30 (4 rounds)

**Rnd 67:** (3 sc, 1 dec) × 6 [24]

**Rnd 68:** (1 sc, 1 dec) × 8 [16]

**Rnd 69:** 8 dec [8]

Finish stuffing the Whale. Fasten off with the inverted magic ring.

### TAIL (MAKE 2)

With **Dark Teal**.
**Rnd 1:** 6 sc in magic ring
**Rnd 2:** 6 sc
**Rnd 3:** (1 sc, 1 inc) × 3 [9]
**Rnd 4:** 9 sc
**Rnd 5:** (2 sc, 1 inc) × 3 [12]
**Rnd 6:** 12 sc
**Rnd 7:** (3 sc, 1 inc) × 3 [15]
**Rnd 8:** 15 sc
**Rnd 9:** (4 sc, 1 inc) × 3 [18]
**Rnd 10:** 18 sc
**Rnd 11:** 1 sc, 1 inc, (2 sc, 1 inc) × 5, 1 sc [24]
**Rnd 12:** 24 sc
**Rnd 13:** (3 sc, 1 inc) × 6 [30]
**Rnd 14:** 30 sc
**Rnd 15:** 2 sc, 1 inc, (4 sc, 1 inc) × 5, 2 sc [36]
**Rnd 16:** 36 sc
**Rnds 17–26:** 36 sc (10 rounds)
**Rnd 27:** (7 sc, 1 dec) × 4 [32]
**Rnds 28–29:** 32 sc (2 rounds)
**Rnd 30:** 3 sc, 1 dec, (6 sc, 1 dec) × 3, 3 sc [28]
**Rnd 31:** (5 sc, 1 dec) × 4 [24]
Pinch the Tail closed with 12 sc. Leave a long tail and do not stuff these pieces.

### FINS (MAKE 2)

With **Dark Teal**.
**Rnd 1:** 6 sc in magic ring
**Rnd 2:** 6 inc [12]
**Rnd 3:** (1 sc, 1 inc) × 6 [18]
**Rnd 4:** 18 sc
**Rnd 5:** 1 sc, 1 inc, (2 sc, 1 inc) × 5, 1 sc [24]
**Rnd 6:** 24 sc
**Rnd 7:** (3 sc, 1 inc) × 6 [30]
**Rnds 8–12:** 30 sc (5 rounds)
Leave a long tail. Do not stuff the Fins.

## BELLY

With **Snow White**. Make 5 chains and from the second chain from the hook make:

**Rows 1–2:** 4 sc, chain and turn (2 rows)

**Row 3:** 1 inc, 2 sc, 1 inc, chain and turn [6]

**Row 4:** 6 sc, chain and turn

**Row 5:** 1 inc, 4 sc, 1 inc, chain and turn [8]

**Rows 6–7:** 8 sc, chain and turn (2 rows)

**Row 8:** 1 inc, 6 sc, 1 inc, chain and turn [10]

**Rows 9–10:** 10 sc, chain and turn (2 rows)

**Row 11:** 1 inc, 8 sc, 1 inc, chain and turn [12]

**Rows 12–13:** 12 sc, chain and turn (2 rows)

**Row 14:** 1 inc, 10 sc, 1 inc, chain and turn [14]

**Rows 15–16:** 14 sc, chain and turn (2 rounds)

**Row 17:** 1 inc, 12 sc, 1 inc, chain and turn [16]

**Rows 18–22:** 16 sc, chain and turn (5 rows)

**Row 23:** 1 inc, 14 sc, 1 inc, chain and turn [18]

**Rows 24–27:** 18 sc, chain and turn (4 rows)

**Row 28:** 1 inc, 16 sc, 1 inc, chain and turn [20]

**Rows 29–30:** 20 sc, chain and turn (2 rows)

**Row 31:** 1 inc, 18 sc, 1 inc, chain and turn [22]

**Rows 32–34:** 22 sc, chain and turn (3 rows)

**Row 35:** 1 inc, 20 sc, 1 inc, chain and turn [24]

**Rows 36–56:** 24 sc, chain and turn (21 rounds)

**Row 57:** Skip 1 st, 21 sc, skip 1 st, 1 sc, chain and turn [22]

**Row 58:** Skip 1 st, 19 sc, skip 1 st, 1 sc, chain and turn [20]

**Row 59:** Skip 1 st, 17 sc, skip 1 st, 1 sc, chain and turn [18]

**Row 60:** Skip 1 st, 15 sc, skip 1 st, 1 sc, chain and turn [16]

**Row 61:** Skip 1 st, 13 sc, skip 1 st, 1 sc, chain and turn [14]

**Row 62:** Skip 1 st, 11 sc, skip 1 st, 1 sc, chain and turn [12]

**Row 63:** Skip 1 st, 9 sc, skip 1 st, 1 sc, chain and turn [10]

Work sc around the whole Belly and leave a long tail.

## ASSEMBLY

Place pins before sewing any part of the Whale.

Sew the Tails between rounds 55 and 66 on the sides of the Body.

Sew the Fins on the sides of the Body, above the Belly, between rounds 35 and 49.

Sew the Belly on the bottom of the Whale.

Contour the bottom part of the eyes with **Snow White**.

# Tips, Tricks, and Techniques

# Before You Begin

## IMPORTANT NOTES WHEN CROCHETING AMIGURUMI

Remember that the complexity of a crochet pattern can vary depending on individual experience. This book includes not only the pattern instructions but also helpful tips, step-by-step photos, and QR codes for additional guidance. As you progress through the projects, I may reference techniques introduced in earlier patterns.

Progress at a comfortable pace and refine your skills through practice. In the world of amigurumi crochet, there are no hard rules. Over time, each crafter develops their personalized approach that suits their style and comfort.

## YARN AND CROCHET HOOK

For all the characters in this book, I opted for cotton fingering yarn paired with a 2.0 mm crochet hook. Cotton is a popular choice for amigurumi due to its ability to create sturdy and long-lasting items, and it's my preferred fiber for these qualities.

Switching to a different type or weight of yarn and crochet hook will alter the size of your completed figure. For instance, using an acrylic worsted yarn with a 4.0 mm crochet hook will result in a much bigger and fluffier item compared to what's illustrated in this book.

When it comes to choosing the best crochet hook, keep in mind that your hook should glide smoothly through stitches without too much resistance. If your stitches are too tight it may mean that you are using a hook that is too small, and you may want to go up a hook size. On the other hand, if there are large gaps in between stitches, you may be using a hook that is too large, and you may want to go down a hook size.

| US | Metric |
|---|---|
| B-1 | 2.25 mm |
| C-2 | 2.75 mm |
| D-3 | 3.25 mm |
| E-4 | 3.50 mm |
| F-5 | 3.75 mm |
| G-6 | 4.00 mm |
| 7 | 4.50 mm |
| H-8 | 5.00 mm |
| I-9 | 5.50 mm |
| J-10 | 6.00 mm |
| K-10.5 | 6.50 mm |
| L-11 | 8.00 mm |
| M-13 | 9.00 mm |
| N-15 | 10.00 mm |
| P-16 | 12.00 mm |

# Finishing Your Piece

STUFFING YOUR AMIGURUMI

For most parts of the amigurumi, like the head and body, I recommend stuffing them as you gradually crochet. For some parts, there will be specific information regarding stuffing to achieve the correct result, like not overstuffing the feet if you want your toy to stand on its own.

Stuffing significantly influences the final shape of your amigurumi, and finding the right balance is crucial. Overstuffing can make your toys appear bloated and stretch the fabric, causing the stitches to open. On the other hand, because polyester stuffing tends to settle over time, insufficient stuffing might lead to a deflated appearance eventually.

Tear the stuffing into smaller pieces rather than trying to stuff a big piece in all at once. This will help keep it from looking clumpy.

Make sure the stuffing reaches into all of the corners and edges, so the piece will maintain the correct shape.

For smaller or narrower pieces, use the back end of your crochet hook or a pair of tweezers to push small amounts of stuffing where they need to go.

GIVING EYES DIMENSION

Use white embroidery yarn to indent the eyes of the amigurumi. Pass the tapestry needle through any stitch on the side of the piece to the bottom of the eyes. Outline the eye with the thread, inserting the needle into the top of the eyes, returning with the needle to the same stitch where you started. Pull the two strands and tie a knot with them. The more you pull the strands, the more indented the eye will be.

## FASTENING OFF AND HIDING THREAD

To hide the remaining thread whenever you are sewing or embroidering, I use two techniques:

1. Invisible knot: Using the yarn in the same color, grab on loop of any stitch next to where the yarn is. Pass the tapestry needle in it and tie a knot. Insert the tapestry needle again in the same gap close to where the yarn is, and pull it so the knot enters the amigurumi. Cut the remaining thread.

2. If there are two ends of the thread (when sewing the ears for example): Insert the tapestry needle in the side of the head and start embroidering. After you embroider the eyes, go back with the tapestry needle to exactly the same place where you started and tie a knot. With the help of the tweezers, push the knot inside the amigurumi.

## GLUING YOUR AMIGURUMI

In sections of your amigurumi that require gluing, opt for a craft glue that dries clear and is suitable for the materials you're working with. The quantity of glue needed will vary based on its strength, but generally, a small drop is sufficient. Be cautious not to over-apply, as excessive glue can seep out and damage the appearance.

## WEAVING IN ENDS

For pieces that are stuffed, you'll simply have to use your hook to pull the ends to the inside of the piece. For pieces that are not stuffed, you will need to use your tapestry needle to work the ends back and forth through the nearby stitches to secure them in place before trimming them.

## CROCHETING PIECES TOGETHER

Many of the patterns in this book involve crocheting pieces together (legs are crocheted with the body). Be sure to crochet the pieces in the correct order so that you'll be able to attach them at the appropriate time.

## JOINING LEGS TOGETHER

For all human-shaped amigurumi in this book:

1. Crochet the left leg completely and fasten off. Then crochet the right leg using the same instructions (do not fasten off).

2. Before joining the legs, crochet a few extra stitches on the right leg. These stitches are important because they help you reach the inner side of the legs, ensuring that when the legs are joined, both feet face forward.

3. Once you reach the side of the right leg, chain the number of stitches indicated in the pattern. (The number may vary depending on the character.)

4. Insert your hook into the left leg and make 1 sc to attach the chain to it. Usually the attachment point is around the third-to-last stitch of the left leg, but this may vary depending on your crochet tension. The most important thing is to attach in a place that keeps both feet pointing forward.

5. On the next round, crochet around both legs, including the stitches of the left leg, the right leg, and the chain you created between them. This forms the beginning of the body.

ATTACHING THE HEAD TO THE BODY (ARTICULATION)

For all human-shaped amigurumi in this book:

Follow the instructions for stuffing the head until the round indicated. Starting with the next row:

Blo 20 sc

20 sc (8 rounds)

10 dec [10]

Fasten off with an inverted magic ring.

Push the neck inward with the help of the hook handle.

Using a tapestry needle attach the head to the body, pass the remaining tail of the head and the remaining tail of the body to the middle of the magic ring that started the head.

Pull the two ends in order to adjust the head to the body, tie a knot and cut the tails. This way, the head will be articulated.

### SEWING PIECES TOGETHER

While many of the patterns in this book have elements that can be crocheted together, they all require a fair bit of sewing as well. Sewing crochet pieces together can be tricky and can have a massive impact on the final result, so it's important to set yourself up for success.

Always leave a sufficient length of thread for sewing, not too short to handle, but avoid cutting an excessively long piece that might lead to wastage.

TIP 1: Wrap the yarn twice around the crochet part that you will attach. Ensure that it is not overly tight, which may cause it to be short. This length is usually enough to sew pieces together.

TIP 2: Use pins to keep the pieces aligned while you sew, which helps maintain the correct placement throughout the process.

# Stitch Abbreviations

**Ch:** Chain
**Sc:** Single crochet
**Hdc:** Half-double crochet
**Dc:** Double crochet
**Sl st:** Slip stitch
**BLO:** Back loop only
**FLO:** Front loop only
**Inc:** Increase
**Dec:** Invisible decrease
**Sc2tog:** Sc 2 st together
**St:** Stitch/stitches
**Rnd:** Round

## SINGLE CROCHET

Every character in this book is crafted using the X-shaped single crochet, also known as the "yarn under" technique. This method creates stitches that are tighter than those made with the V-shaped "yarn over" technique, resulting in amigurumi that are more compact and rigid.

## US VS. UK TERMS

This book is written using US terminology. If you are more familiar with UK terms, here is a helpful conversion chart:

| US Terms | UK Terms |
|---|---|
| **Sl st**—slip stitch | **Ss**—slip stitch |
| **Sc**—single crochet | **Dc**—double crochet |
| **Hdc**—half-double crochet | **Htc**—half-treble crochet |
| **Dc**—double crochet | **Tc**—treble crochet |

# Techniques and Stitch Glossary

## CROCHET AROUND A FOUNDATION CHAIN

Begin by making a chain of the desired length. This will form the base of your project.

To start crocheting in the round, insert your hook into the second chain stitch from the hook you made. Make sc according to the instructions of the pattern in both sides of the chains. Do not make sl st to join the rounds.

## SLIP KNOT

Make a loop with the yarn. Insert your index finger and thumb through the loop and grab the working yarn (connected to the skein) and pull it through the loop, holding on to the tail. Pull until a knot is formed, insert your hook through the new loop and pull the working yarn to tighten the knot.

## CHAIN

With a slip knot on your hook, yarn over and pull up a loop through the slip knot. Yarn over and pull up a loop through the loop on your hook. Repeat these steps as many times as the pattern calls for.

## MAGIC RING

Make a loop with the yarn, leaving a tail around 4 in. long. Insert your hook into the loop and while holding the loop steady, pull the working yarn through. Keep the working yarn loose while using your hook to grab the working yarn on the other side of the loop and pull it through the loop on your hook. Single crochet into the ring by inserting your hook through the large loop, yarn over and pull the working yarn through, yarn over and pull through both loops on the hook. Single crochet the number of stitches the pattern calls for into the magic ring and then pull the tail tight to close the ring. (If you do not like this method, you can also chain 2 and work the number of single crochet the pattern calls for into the second chain from the hook.)

## SINGLE CROCHET (SC)

Insert your hook through both loops of the next stitch, yarn over and pull the working yarn through the stitch (2 loops on the hook), yarn over and pull the working yarn through both loops on the hook.

## BACK POST SINGLE CROCHET (BPSC)

Insert your hook from back to front of the single crochet from the previous round.

Yarn over and pull the working yarn through from behind the post (you now have 2 loops on the hook). Yarn over again and pull through both loops on the hook to complete the stitch.

## HALF DOUBLE CROCHET (HDC)

Yarn over, insert your hook through both loops of the next stitch, yarn over and pull the working yarn through the stitch (3 loops on the hook), yarn over and pull the working yarn through all 3 loops on the hook.

## DOUBLE CROCHET (DC)

Yarn over, insert your hook through both loops of the next stitch, yarn over and pull the working yarn through the stitch (3 loops on the hook), yarn over and pull the working yarn through the first 2 loops on the hook (2 loops on the hook), yarn over and pull the working yarn through both loops on the hook.

### SLIP STITCH (SL ST)

Insert your hook through both loops of the next stitch, yarn over and pull the working yarn through the stitch and through the loop on the hook.

### BACK LOOP ONLY (BLO)

Work in the back loop of the stitch only: the loop that is farthest from you.

### FRONT LOOP ONLY (FLO)

Work in the front loop of the stitch only: the loop that is closest to you.

### INCREASE (INC)

Make 2 single crochet in the same stitch to increase the number of stitches by 1.

### INVISIBLE DECREASE (INV DEC)

Insert hook through the front loops of the next 2 stitches, yarn over and pull the working yarn through both front loops (2 loops on the hook), yarn over and pull the working yarn through both loops on the hook (crocheting 2 stitches together to decrease the number of stitches by 1).

### COLOR CHANGE

Color changes occur on the last stitch before the desired color will be used. Work the stitch in the old color until 2 loops remain on the hook, then use your hook to pull a loop of the new color through both loops. Tie the tail of the new color to the working yarn of the old color and cut the old color. If the color change occurs on the inside of a piece that will be stuffed there is no need to weave in the ends. If the color change occurs on a piece where the wrong side will be visible, then weave in the ends securely.

### RIGHT SIDE (RS)

When crocheting in the round, the right side is the outside of your project. If you are right-handed, you will be working counterclockwise, if you are left-handed, you will be working clockwise.

### WRONG SIDE (WS)

When crocheting in the round, the wrong side is the inside of your project. You will know if you are working with the wrong side out if you are right-handed and you are working clockwise, or if you are left-handed and you are working counterclockwise. The patterns in this book are all written with the right side facing out; if you are working with the wrong side out, you will want to turn the piece so that it is right-side out.

### FASTEN OFF AND HIDE THE REMAINING THREAD

To hide the remaining thread whenever you are sewing or embroidering, I use two techniques:

1. Invisible knot: Using the yarn in the same color, grab on loop of any stitch next to where the yarn is. Pass the tapestry needle in it and tie a knot. Insert the tapestry needle again in the same gap close to where the yarn is, and pull it so the knot enters the amigurumi. Cut the remaining thread.

2. If there are two ends of the thread (when sewing the ears for example): Insert the tapestry needle in the side of the head and start embroidering. After you embroider the eyes, go back with the tapestry needle to exactly the same place where you started and tie a knot. With the help of the tweezers, push the knot inside the amigurumi.

# Acknowledgments

To my wonderful editor, Karyn, for believing in my work and creativity, and for giving life to yet another dream.

To my amazing husband, Eduardo, who, as always, supported and believed in me, and took care of everything so I could focus on this book. Writing it wouldn't have been possible without you.

To my dear sister-in-law, Rejane, who listens to every struggle and moment of self-doubt, and always has the right words to lift me up.

And to my incredible team of testers Ana Carolina Gradowski, Brigita Tomasović, Deliah Pfeiffer, Evelyn Neris Ribeiro, Falicia M Hand, Lais Pitta, and Mary Ann Manconi, who crocheted, proofread, and tested every pattern in this book with so much care and dedication. You were amazing!

# About the Author

Bianca is an amigurumi designer and craft lover who began crocheting in 2015 as a way to relieve stress from her former job as an Air Traffic Controller in the Brazilian Air Force. After years of crocheting as a hobby, she founded her business, Crocheniacs, which initially focused on selling finished amigurumi and later expanded to include her own original patterns.

A naturally timid artist, Bianca discovered a passion for sharing her knowledge with the crochet community through YouTube videos. Teaching others to crochet and spreading joy through each stitch and amigurumi creation brings fulfillment to her life.

She enjoys challenging herself with a variety of amigurumi designs, experimenting with different shapes, and exploring endless possibilities to bring her ideas to life. Bianca has published three amigurumi books, *Crochet Nativity*, *Funkogurumi*, and *Crochet Amigurumi for the Holidays*, which show a little of Bianca's range of ideas in the amigurumi world, reflecting her creativity and personal style.

She holds a degree in Teaching Portuguese and English, a postgraduate certificate in English teaching methodology, and a Master's degree in Teaching, Learning, and Media Education from Tampere University, Finland. Alongside her experience as an Air Traffic Controller, she worked as an Aviation English Instructor for the Air Force.

In her free time, she enjoys indoor climbing with her husband and cooking.

Website: www.crocheniacs.com
YouTube: www.youtube.com/@crocheniacs
Instagram: @crocheniacs